George M. (George Makepeace) Towle

England and Russia in Asia

George M. (George Makepeace) Towle

England and Russia in Asia

ISBN/EAN: 9783744760140

Printed in Europe, USA, Canada, Australia, Japan

Cover: Foto ©ninafisch / pixelio.de

More available books at **www.hansebooks.com**

TIMELY TOPICS

ENGLAND AND RUSSIA IN ASIA

BY

GEORGE MAKEPEACE TOWLE

AUTHOR OF "MODERN GREECE," "ROUMANIA AND SERVIA,"
ETC.

With Maps

BOSTON
JAMES R. OSGOOD AND COMPANY
1885

PREFACE.

THE purpose of the " Timely Topic" series, of which this is the initial volume, is to supply to the reader, in a compact and convenient form, information concerning interesting topics and events which arise from time to time to occupy the popular mind. Whenever a subject reaches, in public interest, a degree of importance like that at present appertaining to the rivalry between England and Russia in the East, or that of the policy of England in Egypt and the Soudan, it is intended to issue promptly a handy volume, which shall enable the reader to understand the causes, bearings, and course of the event in question.

In the present volume the attempt is made to so present and group the facts relating to the Russian and English conquests in Asia, and the conditions of their antagonistic policies on that continent, as to give the reader succinctly, and without the necessity of hunting up and consulting many works, a clear idea of the reasons why the two great European empires are in collision in the East; and to afford him the materials for forming a judgment on the events resulting from that collision as they proceed.

The subject is certainly one of more than incidental or passing interest. It is well-nigh certain to reappear again and again, until the issue is decided by the final arbitrament of arms. There is an "irrepressible conflict" between England and Russia for commercial and military supremacy in Central and Western Asia; and all the world looks to see it go on until one of these powers decisively triumphs over the other.

G. M. T.

BOSTON, April, 1885.

CONTENTS.

		PAGE
I.	THE ENGLISH IN INDIA	7
II.	THE GOVERNMENT OF INDIA	31
III.	THE MILITARY RESOURCES OF INDIA	42
IV.	THE RUSSIANS IN CENTRAL ASIA	45
V.	THE PEOPLES OF TURKISTAN	77
VI.	MILITARY RESOURCES OF RUSSIA	92
VII.	AFGHANISTAN	97
VIII.	ENGLAND *versus* RUSSIA	109

MAPS.

GENERAL MAP OF INDIA.

RUSSIAN ADVANCE IN AFGHANISTAN.

THE RUSSIAN ADVANCE ON HERAT.

ENGLAND AND RUSSIA IN ASIA.

I.

THE ENGLISH IN INDIA.

THE vast English empire of India, with its population of nearly 200,000,000, and its area of nearly 900,000 square miles, has grown up, in the course of three centuries, from a few small settlements founded on its shores by English traders. A company of London merchants received, in 1600, a charter from Queen Elizabeth, which conceded to them the exclusive right to trade with the East Indies for a period of fifteen years. This charter was renewed, nine years after, by James I.; but this second charter did not limit the right it accorded to a definite period, but reserved to the king the power to cancel it at his will. This was the beginning of the famous East India Company, which continued in existence until 1858.

The first dealings of the company were not with the main peninsula of Hindostan, which now constitutes Victoria's great Oriental empire, but with Java, Sumatra, and other islands lying in the Asiatic seas. The first English factory built on Hindoo soil was that erected at Surat, in 1612. The English were not the first Europeans to thus establish themselves in the Indies. The discovery by Vasco da Gama of the ocean passage to the east by the Cape of Good Hope had been followed by several flourishing settlements by his countrymen, the Portuguese, on the west coast of the peninsula; and the Dutch, who were enterprising and adventurous colonists, had also gained a foothold at various points.

The English, therefore, did not establish their settlements in Hindostan without resistance. Both the Portuguese and the Dutch opposed the designs of the company by force of arms. In

1612 a Portuguese fleet made an unsuccessful attack on the English factory at Surat. The Dutch, however, succeeded in ousting their rivals on some of the islands. In spite of these obstacles the East India Company not only maintained the footholds it had already gained, at least on the peninsula, but slowly and steadily added to them. It established its factories both on the west and on the east coast. In 1640 it built Fort St. George, at Madras; and, twenty-two years later, Bombay fell into its hands, as the result of the marriage of Charles II. with Catherine of Braganza, a princess of Portugal. In the latter years of the seventeenth century the possessions of the company increased, and its advance in prosperity was almost uninterrupted.

In the reign of William III. its career was for a while checked by two causes. A new and rival company was organized in England, which threatened the exclusive privileges of the old; and, about the same time, the Great Mogul, Aurengzebe, became hostile to its settlements in India. The company had already established itself on the River Hooghly, on which Calcutta, the present lordly metropolis of Hindostan, is built. The Great Mogul compelled these settlements to be given up. After a while, however, the Great Mogul was propitiated, and not only were the factories on the Hooghly restored, but a strong fort, Fort William, was erected on the site where Calcutta now stands. Then, in 1702, the old company came to terms with the new; the two were consolidated, and a fresh career of prosperity opened before the association thus formed and strengthened.

In course of time the colonies settled around the factories of the company, and dotting both the west and the east coast of Hindostan, were organized into a sort of government, for order and self-defence. They were ruled by agents appointed by the company; and each had a small mixed military force of Englishmen and natives. The Hindoo soldiers thus enlisted were called, and are still known as, "Sepoys," from the Hindoo word "Sipahi," soldier. Down to the middle of the eighteenth century the East India Company never seems to have thought of obtaining political dominion over any part of Hindostan; nor does the idea of its conquest seem to have occurred to the English home government. The English, indeed, may be said to have drifted, or to have been drawn by the course of events, into the political possession of that splendid dependency. Two principal causes operated to bring this about. One of these causes was the breaking up of the once powerful empire of the Great Mogul into rival and jealous States; the other, the collision between the English East India Company and the French East India Company, which had also acquired footholds on the Hindoo coast.

The principal settlement of this French company was at Pondicherry, south of that of the English at Madras. The French had also stations on the island of Mauritius. The outbreak of the "Seven Years' War" between England and France was the signal for a naval attack by the French governors of the Mauritius and Pondicherry, La Bourdonnais and Dupleix, upon Madras. This settlement was taken and occupied by Dupleix; but the cessation of war between the two nations resulted, soon after, in the restoration of Madras to the English. The rivalry between the companies, however, had only begun. Dupleix was ambitious and enterprising, and coveted the possession of all Southern India.

The Mogul empire was now falling in pieces, and Dupleix began to interfere in the quarrels of the Hindoo princes, who, here and there, had set up separate kingdoms in place of that of the Mogul. He deposed the Nabob of Arcot and the Viceroy of the Deccan, and replaced them by puppets of his own; and for a while Dupleix really ruled a large portion of South-eastern India. The rapid growth of the Frenchman's power was a formidable menace to the English settlements, and the agents of the company made haste to support the heir of the deposed nabob. The fortune of war was at first hostile to the English. A small force sent to relieve Trichinopoly was shut up in that town; and its situation became desperate. It was at this critical juncture that a man of rare genius arose not only to deprive the French of the ascendency they had gained, but to lay the broad foundations of an English empire throughout Hindostan.

Robert Clive, the son of a small English farmer, had been sent out to take service as a clerk of the East India Company, because he was so idle and unruly that nothing could be done with him at home. He was a "ne'er-do-well," whom his father was glad to get rid of by packing him off to the other end of the world. Clive was so miserable during his first years in India that he twice attempted to commit suicide. He was homesick, held himself haughtily aloof from his brother clerks, and fairly detested his work at the desk. He had been taken prisoner at Madras by Dupleix, from whom he had escaped in disguise. He now exchanged his clerkship for a commission as an ensign in a force raised by the company. He soon showed such military capacity that he was chosen to lead 500 men against Arcot, which promptly surrendered to him. Clive was besieged in this place for two months by an army of 10,000 Hindoos, whom he held in check by masterly generalship. At last he was relieved by friendly Mahrattas, and, raising the siege of Trichinopoly, restored the son of the nabob who had been deposed by the French, to the throne of Arcot.

With the rise of Robert Clive began the struggle of the English for political dominion as well as commercial supremacy in India. In a few years Clive was appointed Governor of Fort St. David, and entered upon a career of conquest. His first operations were directed to the overthrow of Surajah Dowlah, the nabob of Bengal. This fierce, cruel and jealous prince, who ruled over the richest of the Hindoo States, had taken and sacked Calcutta, seized 150 English, and had thrust them into a horrible dungeon, called the "Black Hole." He had put others in chains. These barbarous deeds aroused Clive to prompt action. He marched on Calcutta with 2,400 troops, and compelled Surajah to submit to a humiliating peace.

But no peace could be lasting so long as Surajah ruled in Bengal. Clive resolved to depose him. A great battle was fought at Plassey, June 23, 1757, between Clive, at the head of 3.000 men, and the nabob, at the head of full 50,000. The Hindoos were utterly defeated; Surajah was taken captive, and was soon after slain in prison. Then Clive met and dispersed the army of the Great Mogul's son at Patna. He placed Meer Jaffier, a tool of the English, on the Bengalee throne, and this prince in return granted to the English a considerable tract of country. Clive next repulsed and annihilated a Dutch fleet which entered the Hooghly, and soon succeeded in firmly establishing English power on that river.

Further south the English were still in conflict with the French East India Company. In 1758 the French, under the command of Count Tollendal, took Fort St. David and destroyed it. They then advanced upon Madras. But that town successfully resisted their impetuous assault. Tollendal was forced to return discomfited to the French post at Pondicherry. His invasion of the Madras country was the last effort of the French to suppress their English rivals. Two years later Tollendal was completely defeated by Eyre Coote at Wandewash, and this event was speedily followed by the capture of Pondicherry itself by the English. Thus came to an end the French dominion on the eastern shores of Hindostan. The English Company now held undisputed sway at all the great stations along that coast.

The policy of encroaching upon the native princes and states, so vigorously begun and prosecuted by Clive, was actively and almost continuously followed up after his departure from India. The council of the company at Calcutta had become a formidable political as well as military power, with its established codes of law and its largely increased army of well-disciplined troops of mixed English and Sepoys. The Great Mogul, whose empire had been shattered into fragments, but who cherished a lingering hope of restoring it, marched against the English in Bengal with 50,000 men, only to be ignominiously routed by the company's troops, comprising less than 20,000, under Munroe. But now a state of confusion and corruption had grown up in the affairs of the company, and Clive was once more summoned to India.

Clive's return was the signal not only for energetic reforms in the company's administration but for renewed encroachments upon the power of the native princes. He promptly brought the Great Mogul and the Nabob of Oude to terms. Restoring the latter to his authority in Oude, on condition that he would remain subject to English influence, Clive persuaded the Mogul to give up to the English the three great provinces of Bengal, Orissa, and Bahar, in consideration of an annual subsidy of £260,000. Clive's efforts to reform the disordered affairs of the company were equally vigorous, and were for a time successful. He put a stop to the private trading of the company's servants, and to their acceptance of bribes from native rulers. He also suppressed with strong arm a mutiny among the company's troops at Monghir.

But when, in 1766, Clive finally returned to England, the disastrous effects of his absence were speedily felt. A conflict took place with

Hyder Ali, the warlike Rajah of Mysore, in which neither side won any signal advantage. A terrible famine spread over north-eastern Hindostan, which swept away a third of the population of Bengal. Meanwhile the affairs of the company, no longer guided by the administrative genius and resolute will of Clive, went from bad to worse. Cruelty, oppression, greed, perfidy and misrule marked many of the proceedings of the English. The reforms achieved by Clive were lost sight of, and corruption and disorder again ran riot among the settlements.

At last the British Parliament, for the first time, was compelled to seriously interfere with the powers and status of the East India Company. A law, proposed by Lord North, was passed in 1773, by which the three great settlements — or "presidencies," as they had come to be called — of Bengal, Madras, and Bombay, were combined under a "Governor-general" of India; a council of four members was appointed to act as the Governor-general's advisers; and a Supreme court of justice was established at Calcutta, that town being designated as the capital of all the Indian dependencies. At this time the Governor of Bengal was a man destined to become world-famous — Warren Hastings; and he was selected by the company as the first Governor-general of India.

The rule of Warren Hastings in India covered a period of eleven years. He assumed office as Governor-general in 1773, and he returned finally to England in 1784. In extending and supplementing the task of bringing the peninsula under English sway he followed vigorously in the footsteps of Clive. Both in his military and in his civil administration Hastings revealed wonderful ability, persistency, and courage. A large portion of his official term was occupied by his wars with native princes. A league was formed by the various Mahratta tribes, supported by the Nizam of the Deccan and Hyder Ali, Rajah of Mysore, to attack the English at Bombay on the west, and Madras on the east. After a long struggle, Hastings made peace with the Mahrattas, without loss of territory or prestige.

Hyder Ali, of Mysore, still held out. He was

the most obstinate and most formidable foe of the English. He threatened Madras, and at first defeated one after another the forces which were sent against him. Finally, Sir Eyre Coote confronted him with a well-appointed army; and, although Hyder Ali was seconded by a French fleet and French soldiers, the English general held him at bay. This war came to an end by reason of Hyder Ali's death. His son, Tippoo, who afterwards showed that he inherited his father's powers and hostility to the English, retreated with his army to Mysore, and peace for a while ensued.

The administration of Warren Hastings, although marred by occasional cruelty and crime, was on the whole wise, just, and powerful. He revived the reforms of Clive, improved the method of levying and gathering native taxes, abolished many of the abuses which had sprung up among the English, built on yet broader foundations the British empire in India, did much to improve the condition of the natives under his rule, and left the peninsula in a condition of peace. His spirit penetrated every distant settlement and presidency. He left a code of rules for the guidance of courts which amply confirms his ability as a great law-maker; and he suppressed the vast system of bribery, which Clive had only temporarily arrested. His council of four was almost always opposing him, and throwing obstacles in his way. But Hastings, with his powerful will and his greater knowledge of Indian affairs, overruled them, and carried out his schemes in spite of them. On his return to England, Warren Hastings was impeached before the House of Lords for high crimes and misdemeanors. That impeachment is familiar as a great historic scene and event. Suffice it here to say that after it had dragged its slow length along for nearly five years, Hastings was acquitted, and permitted to rest in peace for the remainder of his days.

Parliament now found it necessary to take vigorously in hand the regulation of what had become a vast Oriental empire. The East India Company could not be allowed to exercise its powers unchecked. Its exclusive powers must be modified. The home government must interfere for the protection of its subjects, of the natives, and of commerce. After an ineffectual attempt to deal with the question by the North ministry, an India bill, proposed by William Pitt, was duly passed into law. This measure established a home "Board of Control," with its location in London, which had power to approve or annul the acts of the Directors of the East India Company. The President of this Board of Control was to be a member of the ministry, and its other members were to belong to the Privy Council. Thus the political administration of India was brought within the sphere of that of England herself. Henceforth, the home government assumed virtual control over the distant dependency.

Under the successors of Hastings — Lord Cornwallis, Sir John Shore, the Marquis Wellesley, Sir George Barlow, Lord Minto, and the Marquis of Hastings — the policy of subjugating the native princes, of extending the limits of English dominion, and of establishing an English system of laws and administration, on the whole steadily continued. In a bitter war with Tippoo, the son of Hyder Ali, Cornwallis succeeded in overcoming that obstinate warrior, and in extending English authority over more than one half of the central kingdom of Mysore. Cornwallis (who was the same Cornwallis who had delivered up his sword to Washington at Yorktown) proved an able and reforming Governor-general. He corrected the abuses of the land tax, and did much to protect the *ryots*, or peasants, from the oppression of the great landholders. In the Marquis Wellesley, too, — the elder brother of the Duke of Wellington, — India secured a very able and vigorous ruler.

Another fierce war occurred during Wellesley's administration. Tippoo proved that although defeated he had not been annihilated. The French, with whom England was once again at war, tried to form a league among the native princes against the dominant race; but they did not succeed. It was in this second war with Tippoo that Wellington won his first military laurels. The final scene of the struggle was the memorable siege of Seringapatam, which was impetuously stormed and taken by the

English. Tippoo himself was slain while fighting with desperate valor at one of the gateways of the fortress. Mysore, the great region of the Deccan, and the Carnatic, now came permanently under English influence and protection.

But now the Mahrattas broke out into renewed resistance to English rule. One of the most brilliant campaigns in the history of British India ensued. Col. Wellesley, afterwards Duke of Wellington, inflicted a tremendous defeat upon the Mahratta chief, Sindia, at Assayi, and Gen. Lake made a progress of unbroken conquest from Sutlej to Delhi and Agra. The result was that the strength of the Mahrattas was completely broken. Under Lord Minto, who became Governor-general in 1807, the English boundary was extended to the River Sutlej, and the islands of Bourbon and Mauritius were wrested from the French, which destroyed the last hold of the French in the Indian seas.

In 1813 a new charter under fresh restrictions was granted to the East India Company. Its exclusive right to trade in India was withdrawn, and that trade was thrown open to all English merchants; while, for the first time, missionaries were allowed to pursue their ministrations in Hindostan. The Marquis of Hastings, who, in the same year — 1813 — became Governor-general, soon found himself involved in wars with the Nepaulese, north of the Ganges, and with the Pindarees in Central India. The English forces, with their native allies, prevailed in both localities. Nepaul was compelled to make such a peace as to relieve the English of any fear thenceforth of their hostility, and, although the marauding Pindarees were aided by the Peshwa, the chief of all the Mahratta tribes, they were finally dispersed, and the River Indus now became the western frontier of the English dominion in India.

The able rule of the Marquis of Hastings confirmed and established the supremacy of the English power in India. He effected many reforms both in the moral and material condition of the semi-barbarous races over whom he held, in most respects, a beneficent sway. For many years the British administration was undisturbed by serious conflict, and the work of consolidating the empire went steadily on. A war with the Burmese was speedily brought to a term by Lord Amherst; and his successor, Lord William Bentinck, succeeded in suppressing the horrible Hindoo rite of the suttee and the murderous sect of the Thugs. Later, Lord Auckland's attack upon the Afghans, resulting in the wholesale massacre of English troops in the Khyber pass, threatened to disturb the rule of the English in Western India; but the prompt action of the next Governor-general, Lord Ellenborough, in promptly punishing the Afghans by taking and sacking Cabool, put an end to this danger.

In the years between 1842 and 1856 Scinde was conquered and annexed to the English dominions. The Sikhs, after a brief but bloody warfare, were subdued, and an English resident and garrison were stationed at Lahore, in the Punjab; the Sutlej provinces and the Jullundur Doab were annexed; Ceylon, the Punjab, Pegu, Nagpoor and Oude came under English supremacy, and a second Sikh and a second Burmese war were successfully fought by the Anglo-Indian troops. In the course of this period, too, many internal improvements were made in the vast empire. Under the rule of the Marquis of Dalhousie, especially (1848-1855), great public works were carried to completion. Uniform and cheap postal services were established; railways were built; telegraph wires were erected; and the execution of justice and the laws was extended through many disordered States and provinces.

The next great event in the history of British India was one of dark and dismal import. In 1857, during the administration of Viscount Canning, the great Sepoy mutiny broke out, followed by a series of frightful tragedies and sufferings. Discontent at English rule, a superstition about cartridges, the intrigues of princes who had been deprived of sovereignty, conspiracy on the part of the Mohammedans, were all alleged as causes of this formidable outbreak. A Sepoy cavalry regiment at Meerut, not far from Delhi, refused to obey orders on parade. The mutineers were promptly imprisoned; but other native troops now rose in revolt, and took possession of Delhi. Their example was followed in various parts of Central India. Nana Sahib, who claimed the rank of Peshwa, put himself at the head of the rising, and took and massacred the garrison at Cawnpore.

The siege of Lucknow speedily followed, and the heroism with which its devoted defenders held out against their savage and swarming foes, until they were at last relieved by the dauntless Havelock, is one of the most thrilling stories in modern warfare. Sir Colin Campbell finally raised the siege of Lucknow, and by the summer of 1858 the area of rebellion, with the exception of Oude, had been recovered. Oude fell early in 1859, and then the retribution of the English fell upon the leading spirits of the revolt. Tantia Toppee, the Mahratta chief, was hanged; and the King of Delhi, the last of the great Moguls, and the last descendant of the house of Timour Tamerlane, was transported, and kept prisoner in Pegu until his death.

The immediate result of the Sepoy rebellion was the direct assumption of the rule of India by the British government itself. By an act of

Parliament which became a law in August, 1858, the Queen of England was declared to be the sovereign of India, and the East India Company, after a wonderful career of two and a half centuries, ceased to exist. A new executive department was created to manage Indian affairs. At its head was placed a Secretary of State for India, who became a member of the English cabinet. Thenceforth, the Governors-general were appointed by the Crown, became known, unofficially, as "Viceroys," and were placed under the orders of the Secretary of State. In 1879 the Queen was formally proclaimed " Empress of India."

It was by the steps which have thus been rapidly traced that the vast and noble peninsula of Hindostan, with its manifold natural productions, its fine manufactures and rich merchandise, its once civilized peoples, its rare mementos of ancient magnificence and power, its superb monuments of extinct glory, came into the possession of the remote little island of Britain; it was thus that a new civilization and a new importance in the world were conferred upon its teeming millions; and that wealth and power have, for many generations, been reaped by the conquering race.

The English methods of conquest in India were often harsh and cruel. In the course of their advance the English committed many acts of severity, injustice, and oppression. But no one can doubt that, on the whole, the English rule in India has been wise and beneficent. It has planted European civilization in an immense Asiatic State, and among 200,000,000 of Asiatic peoples; it has developed the resources of a country abounding in the materials of an almost fabulous commercial wealth; it has built railways, high-roads, telegraphs; it has conferred upon ancient capitals of barbaric empires sanitary systems and artistic beauties; it has spread education, and insured justice everywhere, by well-organized courts of law; it has suppressed many barbarous rites and customs; has elevated the moral and material condition of the natives, and has secured them peace, protection and orderly government.

II.

THE GOVERNMENT OF INDIA.

THE system of government which has been established in India by its English rulers is worth a brief description. It is despotic in character. At the summit of this government is, of course, the Queen of England and Empress of India. Under the sovereign the Secretary of State for India is the ruler of the dependency. But the policy of the Secretary of State in governing the dependency is determined by him in concert with his colleagues, the Prime Minister and other members of the British Cabinet. There is still another power, behind these and superior to them, which has a supreme voice in the government of India, as indeed, of all other dependencies of the Crown. This is Parliament, or rather as a reality it is the House of Commons. The will of Parliament, of which the

Cabinet is the executive agent, finally determines all the policies of the British empire.

The Secretary of State for India is aided in his functions by a council of fifteen members, who are appointed as vacancies arise by himself. A majority of this council must comprise members who have resided for at least ten years in India. These councillors are appointed for terms of ten years. They cannot sit in the House of Commons, and can only be removed by joint vote of both houses of Parliament. The Council for India is charged with the various departments of business connected with the dependency, and for this purpose is divided by the Secretary of State into various committees. A further regulation concerning the Council is that it must meet at least once a week throughout the year, and that a quorum of five members must always be present.

The Governor-general, or, as he is quite as often called, the "Viceroy," is the supreme executive head of the government of India on the spot. He represents there, and stands for, the Empress. He acts under the instructions of the Secretary of State; but, aside from this, his office is almost that of an absolute despot. He is appointed for a term of six years, and his salary is $125,000 a year; besides which, he is allowed a sum of $60,000 a year more, to maintain a condition of state befitting his dignity. The Viceroy is almost invariably chosen from among the British nobility; and wealth, executive experience, and tested ability are regarded as especial qualifications for the post. During the past one hundred years only three Governors-general have been commoners. The present holder of the office is the brilliant and able Earl of Dufferin.

Like the Secretary of State in London the Viceroy in Calcutta has his advisory council. It is a sort of miniature cabinet. To its six members is confided the administration respectively of the finances, foreign affairs, war department, the interior, and the public works of the empire. The commander-in-chief of the Anglo-Indian army is added to the council as an extraordinary member, by reason of his office. The members of the Council are appointed by the Secretary of State, and are thus in a sense independent of the Viceroy. There is also in India what is called a "Legislative Council." This is formed of the members of the executive council described above, and from six to twelve additional delegates, who are appointed by the Viceroy. The function of this body is to make laws and regulations in public session; but of course their acts are subject to the approval of the supreme executive.

Of the three great Indian presidencies,— Bengal, Bombay, and Madras — Bengal is under the direct rule of the Viceroy, who has his official residence at Calcutta, its capital. The other two presidencies are ruled by governors, who, with their councils, are appointed by the Crown, but are under the Viceroy's control. Besides these governors of presidencies, the districts of Bengal, the North-west Provinces, and the Punjab are administered by lieutenant-governors, and those of Oude, Assam, the Central Provinces, and British Burmah, by English officials who are styled " Chief Commissioners," all of whom are appointed by the Viceroy, and are directly responsible to him. All the States of India under British rule are divided into provinces, each of which is administered by a commissioner; and each province is subdivided into districts, over which are placed magistrates (usually called " Collector Magistrates "), assisted by deputy collectors and assistant magistrates. These magistrates usually are judges.

The governmental system of India cannot be comprehended, unless the distinction is borne in mind which exists between the States which are directly governed by the English, and those which are feudatory and dependent, yet which are still presided over by native princes. Of those under direct English government, the principal are the three presidencies, the Punjab, Oude, and the North-west, Central, and Lower Provinces. The chief states governed by native rulers, but under what is called British " protection," — that is, feudatory and really subject to the English,—are the Deccan, Mysore, Rajpootna, Orissa, Baroda, Cutch, Seik States, Cashmere, Travancore, Scinde, and Rewa. The Island of Ceylon, lying off the south-east coast of the Carnatic, is wholly outside the Indian government, and has an administration of its own appointed by the Crown.

The method by which the Viceroy holds in dependence the States still ruled over by native princes is diplomatic rather than direct. At the court of each of these princes is stationed a quasi-diplomatic agent, called the "British Resident." He is established there as the representative of the Viceroy; and his influence with the prince is naturally irresistible. The relations between the dominant and the dependent power are settled by treaties and agreements; not by direct commands. According to the treaties which the princes have signed, their dependence upon the Anglo-Indian government is acknowledged; they are forbidden to make war or peace with each other, or with any other power; to enter into any diplomatic relations whatever; to establish, beyond certain restrictions agreed upon, a military force, or to allow any European to reside at their courts without the explicit consent of the Viceroy. Moreover, the power of dethroning a prince who governs his state badly rests in the Viceroy's hands. Some of the princes do, and others do not, pay an annual tribute into the Calcutta treasury.

The civil service of the Indian empire is established, like that of England, on the system of competitive examinations and promotions by merit and seniority. It is divided into two branches, the covenanted and the uncovenanted civil service. The former comprises the higher civil service of the administration, is composed entirely of Englishmen, and is supplied from those who have passed examinations held in London. The latter service, for the lower grades of civil work, admits Eurasians (half-breeds of English and Indian blood) and natives.

A word may properly be added here with reference to the finances of British India. These are under the control of the Secretary of State at London, and certain parts of the Indian revenue are paid into the English exchequer. The main source of the revenues of India is the land tax. The latest reports show that the revenue of the empire for the year 1884-5 amounted to £70,560,000 ; the expenditure for that year to £70,241,000. Of the revenue stated, the land tax alone yielded nearly £22,000,000. The revenue from other sources shows that opium yielded the highest sum next to the land tax, namely, £8,600,000 in round figures; then came salt, £6,300,000 ; then, excise, £3,800,000 ; and, fourthly, stamps, £3,500,000. The total debt of India, existing in India itself and in England, is £160,000,000.

The English rule in India has been highly promotive of the spread of education among the swarming millions of the Hindoos. Schools for teaching English have been founded in every province throughout the empire, each province having its school director and inspectors. Higher education is supplied by seminaries, colleges, and universities, supported in whole or in part by the state. There are over 100,000 institutions of education in India, of which 100 are colleges of a high grade, and 98,000 are primary schools. The number of pupils is nearly 3,000,000. There are three universities, one at the seat of each presidency, which grant degrees, and contain over 3,000 students. No figures could more strikingly demonstrate the beneficence, vigor, and liberality of the English masters of India in elevating the intellectual standard of the subject races.

Other splendid proofs of the civilizing results of the British rule in India may be found in the development of its commerce and trade, the rapid extension of its railway and postal systems, and the stimulus given to its manufacturing and agricultural industries. It appears that the imports of the empire in 1883-4 amounted to £63,-000,000, and that its exports reached the dazzling figure of £89,000,000. Of these imports and exports over one-half is to be credited to Calcutta and Bombay. Great Britain, to a very large extent, absorbs this huge volume of commerce, exporting into India goods to the amount of over £40,000,000, and exporting from India over £35,000,000. The United States, it is interesting to note, is fourth on the list of nations dealing with India, our exports into India reaching about £1,000,000 yearly, and our exports therefrom, about £3,500,000. Our imports into India are greater than those of Germany, Austria and Belgium combined, and more than double those of France.

The present railway system of India was set on foot in 1869, though projects had been started and some progress in the building of lines made before that period. The State undertook the task in that year, and the great railway lines have been built by State enterprise and expenditure. There are seven of these principal through lines: the Great Indian Peninsula, the Madras, the Oude and Rohilkund, the Scinde, Punjab and Delhi, the South Indian, and the Eastern Bengal. In 1853, only 20 miles of railway were open throughout India. In 1884 there were nearly 11,000 open, while 2,000 more were in process of completion. In 1883 65,000,000 of passengers were conveyed on Indian railways, and the gross receipts footed up $16,400,000. It is not easy to estimate the enormous extent to which this rapid increase in the facilities of transportation have developed the industries and enhanced the material prosperity of the empire.

The postal service of India reveals a similar rapid growth in efficiency and use. The total number of letters, papers and parcels distributed in 1882-3 was 186,620,569. Of these, 168,119,398 were letters and postal cards; 14,075,667 were newspapers; and 4,400,000 were parcels and packages. These were sent through 13,000 post-offices. The postal revenue amounted to £971,000, and the expenditure to £983,000, so that the postal service shows a small deficit. This, however, has steadily diminished from year to year, and the balance will soon be the other way. The mails were carried over 61,000 miles, for the most part still by boats and "runners," — 9,000 miles only of postal transportation being as yet done by the railways. The telegraph wires have been carried over 22,000 miles, conveying in 1883 nearly 2,000,000 messages, costing £625,000, and giving employment to 324 offices.

III.

THE MILITARY RESOURCES OF INDIA.

In view of the possibility that a war may sooner or later arise between Russia and England, in the East, the military strength of the Indian empire becomes a subject of practical interest. What forces can England collect in India itself, with which to oppose by force of arms a Russian advance? The latest report, which gives the total of the Indian armament for 1884–5, states that the British forces garrisoned there comprise 61,500 men. Of these, 11,260 are royal artillery, 4,280 are cavalry of the line, and 45,500 are infantry of the line. The native army, officered mainly by Englishmen, comprises 127,400 men, of whom 103,700 are infantry. The combined British and native force may, therefore, be estimated at about 190,000 men.

But besides this standing army under the commander-in-chief of India, the Hindoo States, feudatory and independent, have forces which combined number no less than 275,000 men, with 3,000 guns; while the Mohammedan States have 75,000. All the native forces, therefore, may be stated at not less than 350,000. Of these forces, Nepaul has 100,000; Hyderabad, 44,000; Cashmere, 27,000; Oodeypore, 20,000; Gwalior, 11,000; Baroda, 15,000; Jeypore, 18,000; Bhurtpore, 11,500; and Indore, 8,000. It is probable that nearly if not quite all of these forces would be at the disposal of England in the event of war with Russia. Such a war would be one of protection and defence to the Indian States themselves. There is every reason to believe that the rulers of the great States of Hyderabad, Baroda, Mysore, Cashmere, infinitely prefer the rule of England to that of the Cossack; and this feeling is evidently almost universal among the lesser native principalities.

Should war ensue, therefore, Great Britain has in reserve, in India itself, a possible force of no less than 550,000 men. It must be added that a large portion of the native soldiers are well disciplined and are good combatants. The Sikhs of the Punjab, for instance, are perhaps the best Asiatic soldiers. They are thoroughly loyal to British rule, and have on many fields demonstrated both that loyalty and their high military qualities. In anticipation of trouble with Russia, and in order to hold Afghanistan secure from encroachments, the English have recently posted an army of 20,000 men and 32 guns at Quettah, in south-eastern Afghanistan, which place commands the Bolan pass to India, and is connected by railway with the valley of the Indus.

IV.

THE RUSSIANS IN CENTRAL ASIA.

THE story of the Russian advance through Central Asia is not a new one; nor is it recently that the suspicions of Great Britain have first been aroused by that advance. For many years Napoleonic wars and French revolutions, the rise of new kingdoms on the ruins of old, wars of Algiers, of the Crimea, of Italy, of Mexico, of Bohemia, of France, civil war in America, Egyptian troubles, quickly succeeding, have cast the events in Asia into a dim background. Even England, especially watchful and jealous as she is of her Oriental empire, has been so busy in other directions as to lose sight of the far-off danger for long intervals. As a fact, Russia has pursued for nearly three centuries her vast schemes of conquest and aggrandizement in Northern and Central Asia. Steadily, almost stealthily, she has crept eastward to the bleak Pacific coast of Kamtchatka, and southward to the fertile slopes of the Thian Shan and the Bedoor Tagh and to the borders of Northwestern Afghanistan; until now her Asiatic dominions comprised more than one-third of the largest of the world's continents.

The sway of Peter the Great, at the beginning of the eighteenth century, included the greater part of Siberia. Whatever may be thought of the authenticity of that great monarch's will, which enjoined upon his successors the ambitious task of long advances southward from Siberia, and the conquest of Constantinople, it is at least certain that Peter's bold and enterprising spirit foresaw the possibility that the Russian dominion would extend even beyond the limits to which it has, in our day, attained. No fact of modern history, indeed, is more stirring and significant than the slow, but ever-steady, persistent, ever-onward encroachment of Russian power, continued for many generations, towards the confines of British India.

A glance at the map of Central Asia—as the

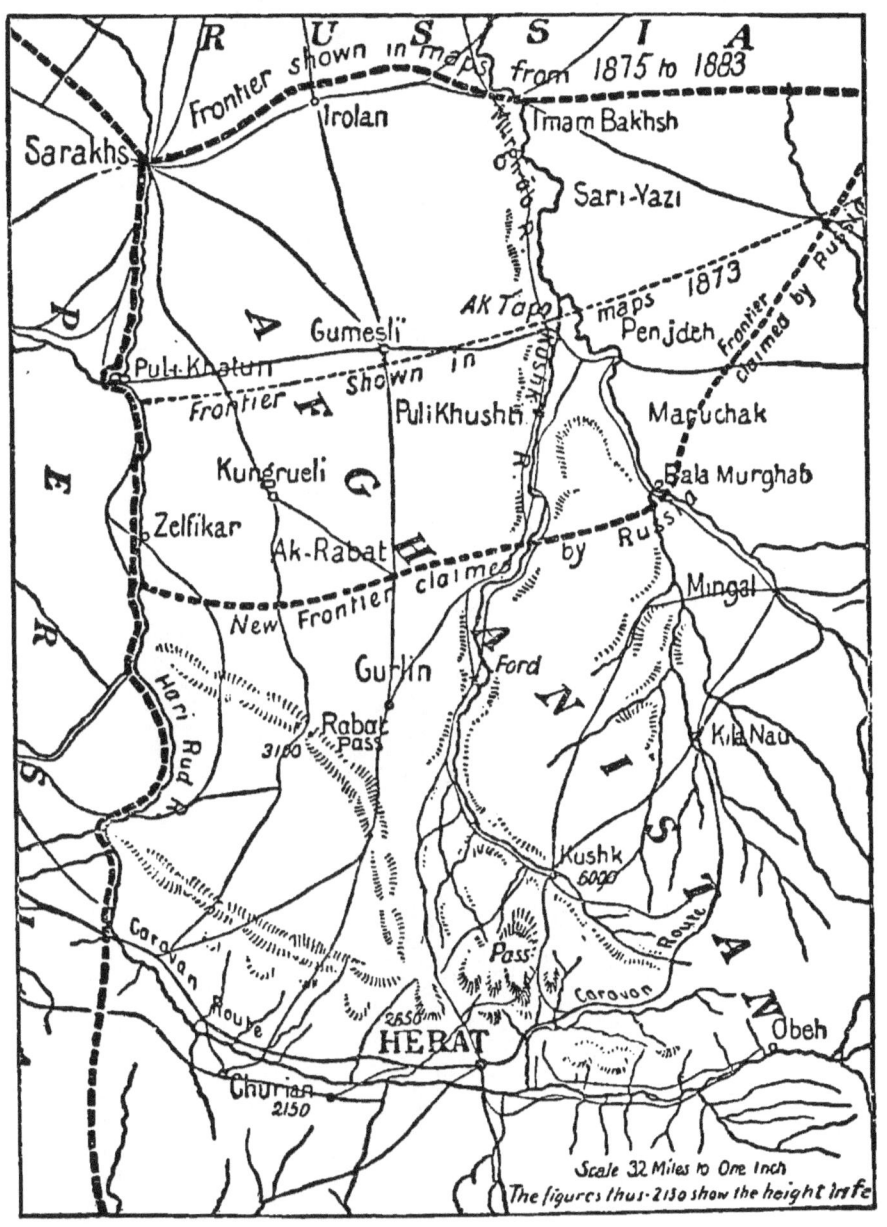

RUSSIAN ADVANCE IN AFGHANISTAN.

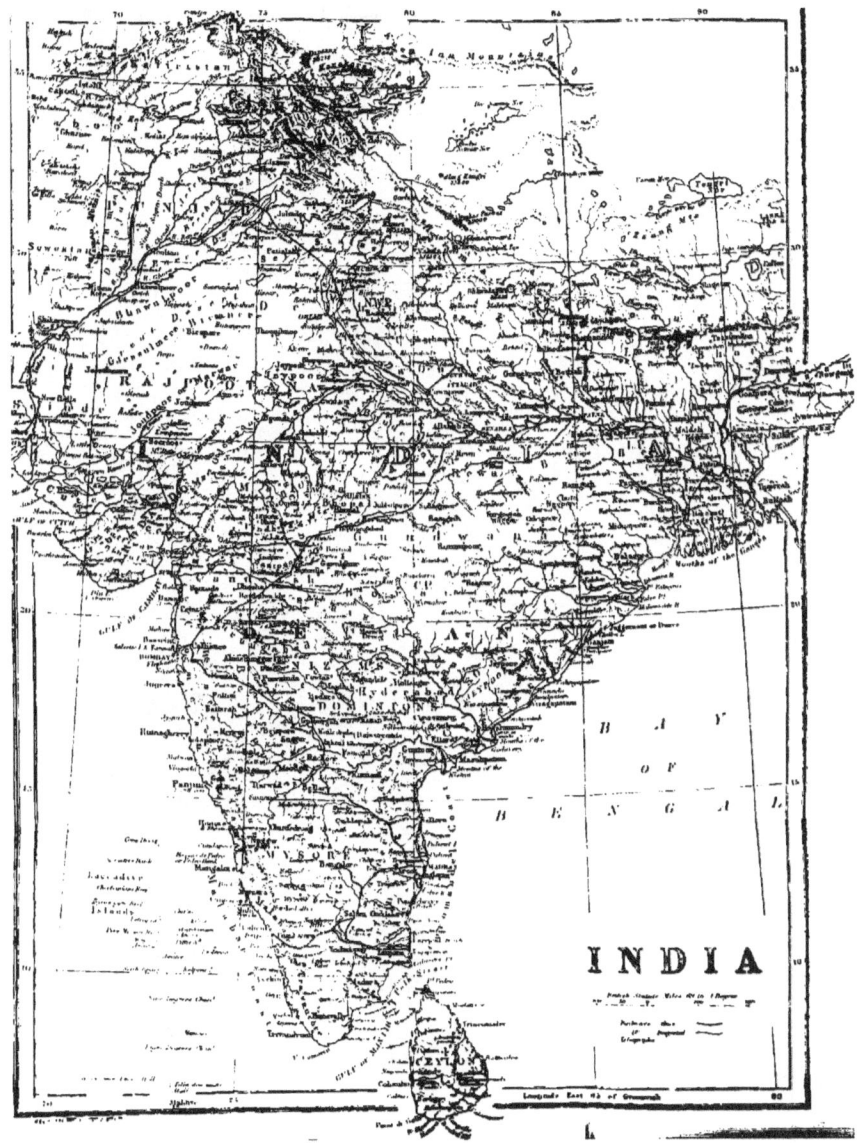

region is vaguely called which lies between Persia and the Caspian on the west, Asiatic Russia on the north, Afghanistan and India on the south, and Kashgar and the Chinese limits on the west,—will at once show what a formidable area the Russians have traversed. They have passed over more than 2,000 miles across dreary wastes and difficult mountain ranges, far beyond the access of railways and telegraphs, into perilous wildernesses peopled by savage and warlike tribes; along the valleys of far-extending rivers, and to the seats of once proud and powerful Asiatic empires; until to-day the Russian outposts are within sight of the giant range of the Hindoo Koosh on the one side, and Russian garrisons occupy Merv and Sarakhs on the other.

The two great rivers of Central Asia, the Oxus and the Jaxartes, are hers throughout almost the entire range of their navigable waters. The two great inland seas of Central Asia, the Sea of Aral and the Sea of Balkash, are also hers. The two ancient historic cities of Tashkent and Samarkand are ruled over by

Russian governors, and are "protected" by Russian troops. The three powerful Khanates of Turkistan — Khiva, Bokhara, and Khokand — acknowledge, though no doubt grudgingly, the supremacy of the White Czar. The Russian soldier has planted his foot on territory which has been supposed to be well within the limits of Afghanistan; and no one can doubt that, so long as the Russian arms are established at Merv, Sarakhs, above the Rabat pass, and in the Murghab valley, there will always exist a danger and menace to the Afghan dominions.

Russia has only been able to make these vast conquests by degrees and at long intervals. Between Semipatalinsk and Akmolinsk, the southernmost of the Siberian provinces, and the rich and fertile Khanate of Khokand, lie the vast and dreary deserts of the "Great" and "Little Hordes" of the Kirghiz. Between the Caspian and the Khivan capital are other deserts, which once, at least, proved a waste too formidable to be crossed even by a well-equipped Russian army. Nature seems to have thrown every difficulty within her resources in the way of the

Russian military progress. Yet by patience, perseverance and repeated effort, Russia has absorbed the Central Asiatic provinces one by one, as the Austrian emperor did the artichoke leaf by leaf, until but two sovereign States, of formidable proportions, separate her dominions from those of Britain in India. These are Kashgar and Afghanistan.

Russia began her long career of Asiatic conquest towards the close of the sixteenth century. Theodore I., who was afterwards poisoned, was Czar of Muscovy, which did not become the Russian empire till more than a century afterwards. Elizabeth was reigning in England, and far from dreaming of the gorgeous Eastern empire over which her successors were to rule, was engaged in defeating Philip's Armada. The first advance was made in the extreme north. Step by step the territories occupied by the nomad tribes of Siberia were absorbed; then the Cossacks of the Don, settled around the northern shores of the Caspian, were conquered; the Ural Tartars were brought under the rule of the Czar; and colonies were established at Perm and other points eastward and south-eastward of Muscovy.

By the close of the seventeenth century the dominion of Russia had stretched completely across the dreary expanses of Siberia, and had included the still more bleak and distant country of Kamtchatka. Peter the Great succeeded to an empire which had become, at least in extent of territory, more Asiatic than European. His sway included the indefinite hordes of Turanian tribes scattered between the rivers Ishim and Irtish and the northern boundaries of Asia. Peter was the most ambitious, the ablest and the most civilized Czar who had ever sat on the Muscovite throne. He formed vast projects of conquest, which comprehended not only that portion of Asia lying between the Caspian and China, but also Constantinople and modern Turkey.

Siberia and the northern shores of the Caspian were Russia's; it remained to extend her dominions to the more fertile south, to cross the great arid steppes occupied by the Kirghiz hordes, and finally to found Russian seats of commerce on the southern Caspian, the Sea of Aral, and even the Persian Gulf and Indian Ocean. Such was the vista of enterprise which the injunction of Peter spread before succeeding Czars. It seemed a gigantic undertaking. It must necessarily be the work of generations. The conquests must be made, as that of Siberia had been made, piecemeal. The progress of Russia in the lines set down by Peter has been indeed slow, painful, interrupted; but on the whole it has been steadily onward. From the time of Peter to that of Nicholas this progress was scarcely perceptible. Catherine II. and Alexander I. found themselves absorbed in European affairs, and had their hands full in the wars which, at brief intervals in the eighteenth century and the early part of the nineteenth, shook the Western continent. The more peaceful era after the final overthrow of Napolean enabled the Czar to prosecute the long-postponed objects of ambition in Asia.

Something had, however, been done between 1750 and 1830 to prepare the way for future operations. A glance at the map of Central Asia will reveal that between the frontiers of

Siberia and Turkistan, there lie vast expanses of steppe and desert, broken but rarely by rivers and mountain ranges, and divided towards the west by the Sea of Aral and a long narrow range approaching it from the north. This desert waste has always been occupied by fierce Kirghiz nomads: on the western side by the Kirghiz of the "Little Horde," and on the east (between Siberia and Khokand) by the Kirghiz of the "Great Horde." It was Russia's task to conquer and obtain unhampered passage across these immense deserts. It was no less an obstacle than this which lay between her and the fruitful promised lands watered by the Jaxartes and the Oxus.

The process by which Russia has finally obtained the mastery of that great region was the same as that employed in Siberia. She began by establishing a line of military posts within easy distance of her frontiers. Then she sent emissaries among the tribes just beyond, who persuaded them to cease from their wandering ways, and under Russian protection and alliance, to settle down in permanent villages. A time would always come when these nearest tribes, threatened by their savage neighbors on the other side, appealed to Russia to defend them; and, before they knew it, they were not only defended but quietly included within the Eastern dominions of the Czar.

Then a further line of military stations would be established, and the contiguous tribes would come, first under Russian protection, and speedily, at a moment when resistance would have been sheer folly, under Russian government. By these means, which required time, but were certain in their operation so long as the strength and treasure of Russia held out, she had reduced by 1830 the Kirghizes of the Little Horde to vassalage. All this was, moreover, so cleverly done as to attach to Russia the real respect and hearty allegiance of the Kirghiz tribes; and this has been an advantage of the utmost importance in the pursuit of her designs farther south.

To bring into clear view the position of Russia in Central Asia forty years ago — since which period her advance has been far more rapid, effective, and alarming to England than had previously been the case — it is necessary to narrate briefly her relations with the great Khanate of Khiva. Khiva, or Khwarizm, finds its limits between the Caspian on the west, the Sea of Aral and the desert of Ust-Urt on the north, the Oxus or Amu river on the east, and Persia and Cabool on the south. It has been the scene of innumerable wars, incursions, revolutions; conquered and reconquered by rival and turbulent tribes; the prize contended for by great chieftains, now of the Buddhist and now of the Mohammedan faith, from Timour Timerlane to Kahim Khan; historic ground, where Alexander's legions are said to have trod; and which, as a necessary *entrepôt* between Asia and Europe, must be held by the power which assumes to control the intercontinental commerce of the future. For a while during the last century, Khiva was governed by Kirghiz rulers friendly to Russian progress; but early in the present century, the Uzbegs, a tribe bitterly and even cruelly hostile to Russia, drove out the Kirghiz "legates," and established over their four tribes princes of their own race, and an Uzbeg Khan over the whole country.

Russia saw the inestimable advantage of getting control of Khiva at the very beginning of her career of Asiatic conquest. Peter the Great tried to subjugate it as long ago as 1717. The country was inaccessible from the side of the Ural, for there the Kirghiz Horde interposed an impenetrable barrier. Peter commissioned one of his generals, Prince Bekovitch, to conquer Khiva. Bekovitch set out from the north-eastern shores of the Caspian, at the head of six thousand men, and after a painful march of nearly three months reached the Khivan oasis. "He repulsed," says an account by a Russian author, "the attacks of the Khivans for three days, but was then deluded into accepting their overtures, and allowed his famished troops to be distributed in small parties among the villages, where hospitality was promised to them. There defence was impossible, and they were nearly all murdered, a few only escaping to tell the tale, and a few lingering on in captivity." Bekovitch himself was flayed alive, and a drum-head was made of his skin. So utterly disastrous was the issue of the expedition, that " to be swallowed up like Bekovitch" is to this day a familiar Russian saying.

The Czars made no further serious attempt to conquer Khiva from that time until 1839; but on several occasions in the eighteenth century its rulers offered allegiance to the Russian crown ; and this fact, indeed, has always since constituted one of the Czar's claims to Khivan sovereignty. In 1839 the celebrated expedition of General Perovski took place. England herself was forced to acknowledge that this expedition was a justifiable one. For many years the Uzbegs had made a practice of obstructing and robbing the Russian caravans, making sudden attacks upon the outposts, imprisoning, torturing and often murdering merchants who were peaceably going their ways of trade, endeavoring to incite the Kirghizes north of them to insurrection against Russian rule, and returning insulting responses to demands for reparation. Thus the Czar's dignity and his aggressive interest coincided in impelling him to undertake the subjugation of the Khivan Uzbegs. His design was hastened by the English expedition into Afghanistan; for now it was clear that Central Asia was to be the battle-ground of Russian and English interests in the Orient.

Perovski set out from the shores of the Caspian on the 29th of November, 1839. His force comprised five thousand men, ten thousand camels of burden and twenty-two field-guns. Of his army, two thousand were cavalry. It was with a force and armament so small that Russia hoped to conquer a country with a fixed population of half a million, and having tributary tribes numbering as many more. One feature of this, as of all the Russian expeditions in the East, is worthy of note and of praise. The preparations for it were ample. Money was not spared to make every appointment complete. The ten thousand camels carried plenty of warm clothing for every soldier, six months' rations for each man, and even many comforts for the protracted camp-life expected in the deserts.

But Perovski, like Bekovitch before him, was doomed to failure. In more than two months he had advanced only four hundred miles, less than half way from the Caspian to the oasis; and here, in the midst of the barren desert, finding that one-fifth of his army and four-fifths of his camels had succumbed to the bitter hardships of winter, and to various diseases, the general resolved to retrace his steps. The retreat was a masterly one, and Perovski was received by Nicholas with almost as much honor as if he had returned a conqueror. His enterprise, indeed, had not been wholly fruitless. His troops had at least one engagement with the Khivans, which so deeply impressed them with Russian prowess that the Khan, fearing another expedition, released the Russian prisoners in his hands, prohibited his subjects from reducing Russians to slavery, and received the Czar's envoys with effusive demonstrations of respect.

Between Perovski's expedition in 1839, and that which, under General Kauffmann, in the winter of 1873, finally reduced Khiva to Russian vassalage, the advance of Russia in other parts of Central Asia was rapid, and well calculated to arouse the fears of England. A comparison of her outposts held in 1839 with those acquired since, down to the present time, clearly indicates how energetic has been the pursuit of her long-cherished ambition during the past forty years. At the former period the bold and historic frontiers of the Caucasus were still independent of Russian rule; and Russia was forced to keep an army of one hundred thousand men to defend her territory from the depredations of the Caucasian tribes.

There were no railways, and Russia but timidly navigated the extreme northern waters of the Caspian with two small steamers. She had just acquired the Island of Ashurada, then only a sand-bank, now one of her most important strongholds in the Caspian. The frontiers of Russia across the continent from west to east found their southern limit in a line of forts and outposts drawn from the Ural river to the ancient Tartar city of Semipalatinsk, on the Irtish, in the south-east corner of Siberia. Thus forty-six years ago Russia was, at the nearest point, fully one thousand miles from the giant range of the Hindoo Koosh, which separates British India from Turkistan.

Now a line of railway connects St. Petersburg and Moscow with the Black Sea, and within the past ten years a railway has been completed between a convenient point on the Black Sea and the Caspian, passing below the spurs of the Caucasus range. Several hundred steamers are constantly afloat on the Volga, and for the past fifteen years Russia has maintained a war flotilla of from fifty to eighty vessels on the Caspian. On the distant and desert-bound Sea of Aral itself there is quite a formidable Russian war fleet, which, since the acquisition of Khiva and the water-roads of the Jaxartes and the Oxus, has been considerably increased. Russian naval stations have been established from time to time on the Persian coast of the Caspian, so that the dominions of the Shah would be completely at the mercy of Russia were it not for the dangers of British hostility. The same may be said of the dominions of the Ameer of Cabool and Afghanistan. Russian troops are to-day within the supposed boundary of Afghanistan; and probably the only motive which has hitherto restrained them from advancing to the conquest of that rich and fertile land, which would open to them the southern seas, is the hesitation of Russia to come into direct collision with England.

Perhaps the most interesting and significant of all the operations of Russia in Central Asia were those by which she has become virtually dominant over the great Khanates of Bokhara and Khokand. Bokhara has always been a chief centre, dépôt, and market of Central Asian trade, and as such has long been coveted by both Russia and England. From the time when, but a generation after Mohammed's death, a Moslem army overran the country, conquering both the Tartar nomads scattered over its wastes and the more civilized Iranese followers of Zoroaster in the settled districts, Bokhara has been almost constantly the battle-ground of Oriental religions, races, and fierce rival ambitions.

When settled under Mohammedan rule, which sought its chief military support not from the primitive Tajiks, fire-worshippers, but from the

Mongol Buddhists, Bokhara about the ninth century reached a high degree of power and even splendor. "It was not only the seat," says a historian, "of a magnificent empire, but the centre of liberal cultivation and learning." Then came the ruthless Jengis Khan with his Tartar hordes, overruning Turkistan from the Indus to the Mesopotamian mountains; and, soon succeeding this warrior, a still greater warrior appeared on the same scene in the person of Timour Tamerlane, who built up a vast and powerful empire, and who lies entombed at Samarkand, the second of Bokharan cities. The descendants of these two chiefs long disputed the sovereignty of the Southern Turkistani States; but finally the grand viziers gained possession of the power, as the mayors of the palace had done in France. The last prince of Bokhara who claimed a descent from Jengis Khan was deposed by his vizier in 1784; and the grandson of that vizier is the present reigning Ameer of Bokhara.

In the contention between Russia and England for the control of Bokhara Russia had the start, and has pursued her advantage with sleepless pertinacity. While Khiva on one side and Khokand on the other have always bitterly resisted Russian influence and progress, Bokhara, jealous of the ascendency which England acquired in neighboring Cabool, rather encouraged Russian projects, with the result of finding herself at last reduced to a state of virtual dependence upon that power. Russia began her designs upon Bokhara by endeavoring to establish diplomatic relations and commercial treaties with the Ameer. Missions were exchanged between the two courts as long ago as the middle of the last century; but the results were not large, and at the proper moment Russia entered upon the project of bringing Bokhara within her military control.

In order to reach Bokhara, however, it was necessary first to subdue the large, formidable and warlike Khanate of Khokand, lying between Bokhara and the Kara Tagh range, and occupying the banks of the Jaxartes down to where it flows into the Sea of Aral. Khokand was long ruled by the descendants of Timour; then it became for a while a dependency of Bokhara; then, under another descendant of Timour, it regained, about a century ago, its independence. The Khans of Khokand extended their dominions by frequent conquests, until they came into collision, in the lower valley of the Jaxartes, with the Khivans and the Kirghiz hordes; and it was their attack upon the latter, who enjoyed the protection of Russia, which gave Russia the excuse and opportunity to assume an aggressive warfare on Khokand.

It was about forty-five years ago, four or five years before the ill-fated Perovski expedition against Khiva, that the Russians established their first military post on the Jaxartes. This river flows into the northern arm of the Sea of Aral, as the Oxus does into its southern arm; and this step was the first of the series by which Russia advanced her frontier line from Orenburg and Semipalatinsk to the wide semicircle stretching from Fort Kopal around the foot of the great southern ranges to the Sea of Aral. At Aralsk, near the mouth of the Jaxartes, she built a fort, and soon after a second fort, some sixty miles distant, farther up the Jaxartes, at Kazaly.

The Russians were now in a position to

defend their vassals, the Kirghiz nomads, from the constant forays of the Khokandis. These latter held as their extreme northern post Fort Ak Masjid, on the Jaxartes, three hundred miles distant from Aralsk. This fort was commanded by Yakub Beg, one of the most remarkable figures in modern Oriental history. Yakub, a foreign adventurer, probably of Caucasian origin, had taken service under the Khan of Khokand, and by the exhibition of rare military capacity had risen to the command of what was the most important outpost of the Khan's recently acquired dominions. It was the same Yakub Beg who lately reigned, with Draco-like severity and with the sternest and most impartial justice, over the great kingdom of Kashgar, which he himself created by conquest.

In 1852 the Russians made their first attack upon Yakub, then commanding the Khokandi fort Ak Masjid; but he repulsed them with heavy loss. In the following year Perovski —the same who had vainly marched against Khiva—led a force of 1,700 men against Yakub, and this time, after a most obstinately fought siege and series of battles, Fort Ak Masjid fell. At almost the same time Russian forces descended from Semipalatinsk on the extreme north-east, and established Forts Kopal, Iliisk, and Vernoë. Thus were acquired the two horns of that vast semicircle by which the Russian frontier has been pushed, within twenty years, more than a thousand miles nearer India and the sea. The progress of the Russians was stayed by the disastrous war of the Crimea; but gradually the Russian lines, from Ak Masjid on the one side and Kopal on the other, drew near each other along the river banks and mountain bases. In 1857 they had established a station at Suzek, at the foot of the Kara Tagh range; two years later they had reached Kastek, and had narrowed the gap on the other side by erecting a fort at Julek.

Finally, by 1864, the Russians had completed their possession of the great semicircular frontier, had brought the neighboring nomads into a not unwilling vassalage, and had contracted the Khokand Khanate to less than half of its ancient dimensions. The capture of Hazrat Sultan, a flourishing town lying between the Jaxartes and the Kara Tagh mountains, and of Chamkand, south of it, soon followed. The next object of assault was the thriving city of Tashkend, which is said to spread over an area of ten miles by five, with very high walls, and fortifications as formidable as Uzbeg science could make them. The first attack upon Tashkend was repulsed with heavy loss to the assailants. The Khokandis swarmed northward, and the Russian occupation of Hazrat Sultan was for a while threatened.

Reinforcements enabled the Russian general once more to assume the offensive, early in 1865; but not until the Ameer of Bokhara had hastened to the assistance of the Khan of Khokand, probably with the real object of getting possession of the beleaguered Khanate for himself. Gen. Cherniayeff laid siege to Tashkend, with its 200,000 inhabitants, with a force of about 2,000 men. The resistance of the Khokandis was obstinate; but the Russians succeeded first in cutting off the water supply, and then in defeating the valiant Khokandi general, Alim Kul, in a *sortie;* Alim himself falling in the battle, and thus leaving Khokand without a single leader of courage and conspicuous ability. The supply of food as well as of water was now cut off from the doomed city, which capitulated after a siege of six weeks.

The capture and occupation of Tashkend may be said to have given the Russians final and well-nigh complete control of the great Khanate of Khokand. They established there not only a large garrison, but a commercial emporium and a civil government; and, at the present moment, a Russian governor and council and Russian courts and police are settled there. It was until recently the centre of all their military operations, and from thence they are able to dictate to the Khan at Khokand, and to protect the upper valley of the Jaxartes.

A new and unexpected foe now confronted the Russian conquerors. This was Musaffar-uddin, Ameer of the powerful State of Bokhara, of which we have before spoken as an important seat of Central Asian trade. This prince demanded that Tashkend should be evacuated;

and when he found that remonstrance was useless he marched against that city with 40,000 soldiers. The Russian general Romanovski advanced to meet him with a force of about 3,000, and finding him intrenched some miles south of the Jaxartes, gave him battle. "The Bokharan artillery," says a narrator, " was numerous and heavy, but, fired over the heads of the Russians, while the Russian shells and rockets filled their camp with carnage and confusion." The result was that Musaffar soon retreated in disorder, leaving his treasure, arms, and camp equipage behind him.

In consequence of this victory the Russians were able to occupy the strongly fortified and commercial city of Khojand, and a little later to advance into that beautiful, fertile and historic valley of Samarkand, where Timour Tamerlane rested from his conquests, died, and still lies entombed. Such were the features and acquisitions of Russian progress in the valley of the Jaxartes. Khokand and Samarkand are virtually subject to the dominion of the Czar. Bokhara, if still nominally independent, has lost some portion of its eastern territory and is held in awe by the Russian troops; while Russian diplomatic agents have a predominating influence at the Ameer's court.

To capture Khiva was a task that still remained after Khokand had fallen. The valley of the Oxus was quite as necessary to Russian projects as that of the Jaxartes. The third and successful Russian expedition against Khiva was undertaken in the winter of 1872–73. It was commanded by Gen. Kauffmann, and consisted of four columns, starting from different points and converging on the desert capital. Two of these columns — one of them accompanied by the commander-in-chief — proceeded eastward across the desert from two points on the Caspian, the most northerly following very nearly in the line taken by Perovski in 1839. The other two columns proceeded southward from the eastern and western banks of the Sea of Aral. In all there were but 4,000 men; and Khiva contained at least half a million inhabitants.

Russia staked her whole prestige in Central

Asia on the issue of this undertaking. If a third failure to capture Khiva occurred, there was little doubt that a general uprising against Russian rule would take place in the valley of the Jaxartes. Success would go far towards finally establishing Russian supremacy throughout Turkistan. So admirable were Kauffmann's plans that the four columns reached the walls of the Uzbeg capital within a few days of each other, the column commanded by the general himself being first on the spot. A short and sharp struggle ensued; the fiery young Khan defended his chief city with pluck and courage, but his utmost efforts were vain. He capitulated, and became the prisoner of Russia; and the city of Khiva was occupied by Kauffmann's troops.

England was thoroughly alarmed by the Khivan expedition, and yet more so when Khiva fell. She demanded of Russia that, when the Khan had been punished for imprisoning Russians, and the safety of Russian caravans crossing the desert had been secured, Khiva should be evacuated. Assurances to this effect were given by a special envoy of the Czar sent to London. A Russian garrison, however, still holds Khiva, and Russian war-ships have long floated unforbidden on the Oxus. By the destruction of the dams which shut the Oxus to navigation there is free passage for the Russian flotilla for hundreds of miles southward, even to within forty or fifty miles of the city of Bokhara itself; while navigation on the Jaxartes is possible to within the same distance of Sámarkand on the other side. The Russian stations on the Caspian, the two great rivers, and the Sea of Aral now sustain each other in a great cordon of military, naval, and river bases; and Russian power makes itself directly felt on the frontiers of Persia, Bokhara, Afghanistan and Kashgar.

The complete control of Turkistan, east and west, may now fairly be said to be in the hands of the Czar's troops, governors, and emissaries. In 1884 another significant advance of the Russian forces took place. Passing the left bank of the Oxus — an act which England had once threatened to consider as a *casus belli* — they occupied the famous oasis of Merv, and set up a government in that important *entrepôt* and fortress. Merv is one of the military keys of the desert region which borders upon the confines of Khorassan, in Persia, and its occupation by Russia was an event of serious import in the process of absorbing and dominating Central Asia.

But Merv was not the limit of Russian aggression in 1884. The Russian outposts were carried farther still to the south-westward, and occupied the town of Sarakhs, which is also a military position of strategic value, and which stands as near as possible at the junction of the three frontiers of Turkistan, Persia, and Afghanistan. The importance of Sarakhs to the Russian scheme of conquest lies to some extent in the fact that it enables Russia to carry forward her railway from the Caspian and Askabad, now in rapid process of building, to the regions on which she looks with a specially covetous eye.

Towards the end of 1884 the Russian lines were extended still farther southward, and now entered the valleys of the Murghab and Heri rivers, within the boundaries of what has hitherto been regarded as the territory of Afghanistan. One detachment advanced from Sarakhs into the valley of the Heri to the Zulfikar ravine, and thence to Akrabat. Another proceeded from Merv up the right bank of the Murghab to Sari-Yazi, and even pushed an outpost as far as Kishti. Meanwhile the Ameer of Afghanistan pushed his outposts up to Penj-deh, also on the Murghab, and directly confronted the Russians at that point. The English commissioner, meanwhile, took up his head-quarters with his escort at Gul-ran, to the south of Akrabat.

The aggressive operations of Russia in 1884 aroused England to energetic diplomatic action. The boundaries between Afghanistan, Persia, and the Merv district have never been authoritatively settled and agreed upon. England proposed to Russia that commissioners from each empire should proceed to that vague region and finally determine the line which should mark the dominions of the Afghan Ameer. This was agreed to, and the commissioners were appointed. Sir Peter Lumsden, the English commissioner, went to the disputed country; but the Russian commissioner held back; and during this delay the complications between England and Russia, as a consequence of the advance of the latter into the valleys of the Heri and the Murghab, arose.

The immediate cause of the alarm and sudden promptitude of England has yet to be stated. Less than a hundred miles south of the Russian outposts at Zulfikar and Akrabat stands the most formidable fortress and most commanding military site in Central or Western Asia. This is Herat. Herat may be called the Ehrenbreitstein, the Gibraltar of the territories in the midst of which it is situated. It has been traditionally called " the Gate of India." It can be approached from the north through the Rabat pass; and the Russians, at Akrabat, were within two days' march of the Rabat pass. The Russians once in possession of Herat, India would be distinctly menaced. Herat commands all the valleys leading from Persia and Western Turkistan into Afghanistan. In Russian hands it would be well-nigh impregnable, especially should the trans-Caspian railway be completed to its walls. The supreme military importance of Herat requires that a more full description should be given of it; and this will be found in a subsequent chapter on Afghanistan,[1] within whose territority Herat is indisputably included.

---

[1] Page 103.

V.

THE PEOPLES OF TURKISTAN.

It is worth while to consider briefly the character of the races which, in their long career of Central Asian conquest, the Czars have virtually added to their already enormous empire; and the general results of the substitution of Russian rule for the almost chronic anarchy, which, before the arrival of the Russians, prevailed in the Khanates of Turkistan.

As the Russians began their progress southward from Orenburg and eastward from the Caspian, they first encountered the great nomadic tribe of the Kirghiz. This strange, wandering people, Mohammedan in faith, Turkish, probably, in origin, and once forming a powerful and warlike nation comprising several millions of people, which carried its conquests as far south as Tashkend, are divided into vast "Hordes," and tend their flocks and herds amid the solitudes of the desert and the steppe. In all the "Hordes," of which there are four, the Kirghiz probably number between twelve and thirteen hundred thousand. They are described as speaking a tongue much resembling the Tartar, while their physiognomies are a curious mixture of Turk and Mongolian. They have intermarried extensively with women of Western China, which probably accounts for their partial resemblance to the Mongolian type.

"The Kirghiz," says Mr. Schuyler in his "Turkistan," "are in general short of stature, with round swarthy faces, insignificant noses, and small, sharp black eyes, and the tightly-drawn eyelid which is seen in all the Mongol tribes." The Kirghiz lives in a tent made of light felt, with a felt flap for a door, a fire in the middle, and the sides of the tent decked with ribbons. Sometimes, however, he prefers an underground hut, wherein his family, his calves, and his dogs eat, sleep, and while away the time together. Around his

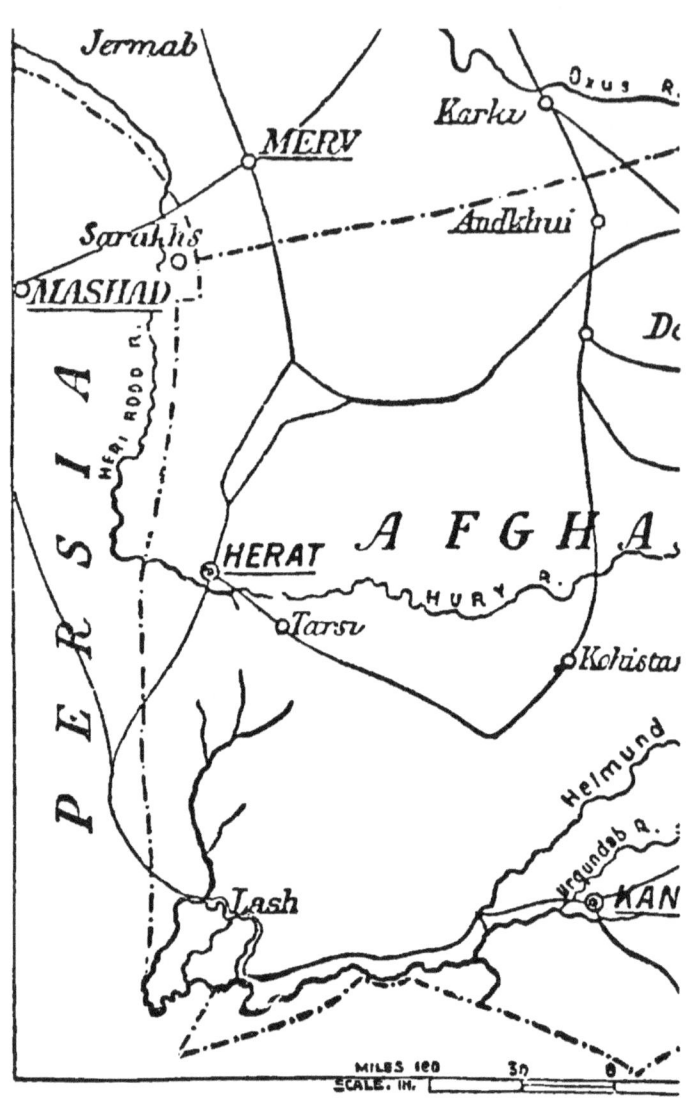

THE RUSSIAN A

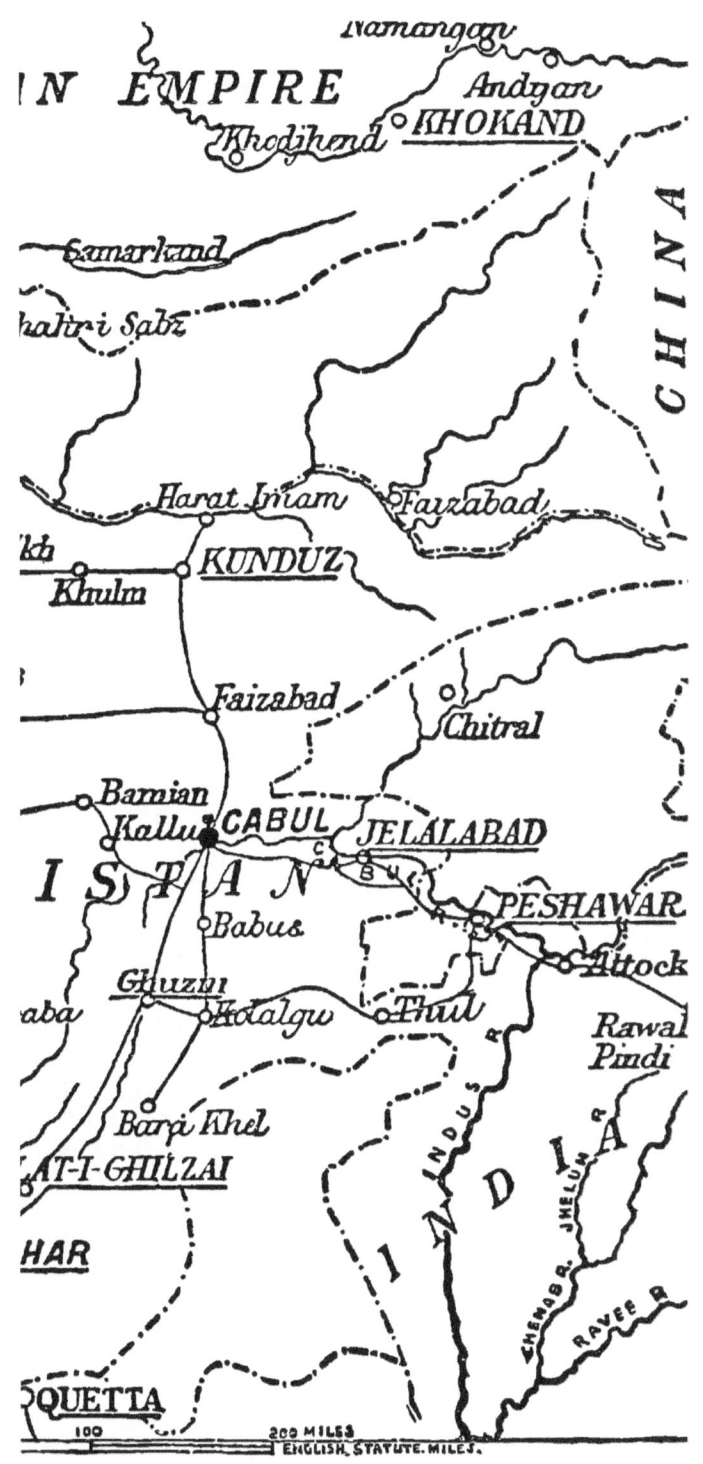

THE RUSSIAN ADVANCE ON HERAT.

tent or hut he hangs his carpets and clothing; and when he is rich, you may also see his silver utensils and the trappings of his horses dangling from the felt. He shaves his head close, and wears what beard nature vouchsafes to him. For clothing, he is content with one or two very simple garments. A pair of baggy breeches and a rough shirt with a very large collar are enough for the ordinary class of Kirghiz. But these nomads have their aristocracy. The Kirghiz nabob is often a very magnificent fellow, displaying his wealth upon his person with gold-embroidered velvet cloaks, and skull-caps richly laced, and silver-mounted belts; while his horses are adorned with equally elaborate saddles and bridles, in which gems as well as gold and silver glitter.

The Kirghiz women wear loose jackets and trousers, and, like other Mohammedan women, are curiously swathed about the head and neck with cotton folds. The Kirghiz young girls wear their hair closely cropped behind, while in front it flows down long and is plaited into graceful braids. "The women," Mr. Schuyler tells us, "spin, embroider very well, cook, and do most of the work — as the men are too lazy to do more than look after their horses." The Kirghiz is, it seems, a shiftless and improvident person; he goes without drink for a day, and without food for several, and then gorges himself to stupidity. He eats mutton and horseflesh, and is prodigiously fond of tea; being content, however, with a very poor quality of that beverage. He also stupefies himself with a strange drink composed of fermented mare's milk.

The Kirghiz is as slack in his religion as he is shiftless in his vocation. It is to be feared that the Prophet would scarcely recognize the rites, and he certainly would be loath to accept the superstitions, of his Kirghiz followers. Their Mohammedanism is as vague and as little spiritual as the Christianity of the Montenegrin peasants. A stranger meeting a group of Kirghiz astride of their horses on the steppe is more terrified than there is need at their wild and swarthy appearance. He is, in truth, on better acquaintance, a not unamiable and very childlike person. He is superior, indeed, to all other Central Asian races. He is generous, hospitable, social; credulous, yet not himself very punctilious as to telling the truth; fickle and easily persuaded; timid in war, preferring scout-duty to service at the front; a marauder when he has a chance, but never wantonly murderous. He delights, above all, in his horses, and is most happy when on horseback; indolent when on the ground, he is no sooner astride his steed than he can travel great distances without weariness. The Kirghiz, too, is fond of music, and sings a great deal; and no singing people can be utterly depraved. There is a Kirghiz poetry; and the favorite instruments are the guitar and the drum.

Very different from the races of the great and little hordes of the steppes and deserts are those which swarm in the cities and towns farther south, on the upper waters of the Jaxartes and the Oxus, and in the Khanates of Khokand and Bokhara. Here we come upon thriving emporiums and busy marts, and sometimes noble monuments of Asiatic architecture and ancient civilization. Tashkend and Samarkand are the two most important cities of Turkistan which have fallen under Russian sway. Tashkend is in many respects the most interesting. There is a Russian town and a native town, and the latter presents on every hand the varied aspect of a settlement that has been built up during many ages by various races. The streets are tortuous; the town is everywhere adorned by gardens; and the walls of the city, celebrated in its sieges, are sixteen miles long, and from twelve to fifteen feet high.

Lovely gardens adorn the suburbs beyond the walls. The houses are neat, white buildings, and the Russian town, at least, is supplied with many European and all the Asiatic luxuries. The population of the city is stated at somewhere in the vicinity of 120,000. This population includes a curious variety of races, and in this respect Tashkend somewhat resembles Bombay. First and most numerous are the Uzbegs, a people who are very numerous throughout Central and Southern Turkistan. Then there are the Tajiks (of Persian origin), and some Kirghiz, Tartars,

Jews, and Hindoos. The Uzbegs, like their more restless neighbors, the Kirghiz, are the descendants of Turkish tribes who wandered from the west into the upper valley of the Jaxartes centuries ago. They are divided into clans, each clan comprising a family with its near and remote degrees of relationship.

The Uzbeg regards his race as the aristocratic one, and he holds all the other races in contempt. He is usually tall and rather gaunt, with a long and expressively sober face. The Tajik, on the other hand, is stocky and full in form, with long black beard, and sly black eyes. He is far less thrifty and industrious than the Uzbeg, and is a poor worker and an apt liar. But while the races are very different in character, their customs and even dress are similar, and some familiarity with the community is necessary before they can be distinguished. The men of Tashkend, like the Kirghiz, wear long baggy trousers, bound to the waist with a girdle or belt, over which they wear a loose gown extending to the ankles, with long, loose sleeves, — a garment much like that worn by the Parsees. Around the waist a scarf is sometimes worn, sometimes a shawl; the Jews resident in Tashkend must use cords as girdles, this being a sign of ignominy.

A very complicated affair is the turban with which the denizens of the city burden their heads, requiring much skill to wind it around the cranium so as to make a presentable appearance. The priests wear white turbans, but the merchants prefer more showy colors. As for the women, they dress not unlike their lords, except that, as is the case with the gentler sex everywhere, they wear bright and varied tints. Like all Asiatic women those of Tashkend are extravagantly fond of personal decoration. They wear a profusion of necklaces, ear-rings, pendants in the hair, and now and then a swarthy damsel is to be observed with a ring in her nose. The Mussulman custom of veiling themselves closely when in the street is maintained by the women of Tashkend, though it is observed that their curiosity often gets the better of them, and they are fain to take a sly peep at the Europeans as they pass. This is, however, a very venial sin, as it is not so wicked for a woman to let her face be seen by an infidel as by one of the faithful.

The favorite articles of food throughout Turkistan are rice and mutton made into a sort of stew, which is eaten with the hands. The people of Tashkend are not horse-eaters, as are the Kirghiz. Like the Kirghiz, however, they are exceedingly fond of tea, and drink it at all hours of the day. Wine is quite unknown; but the Russians have taught the Tashkendis the unwholesome fascinations of "fire-water." They have a sort of beer, too, made of grain, called *buza*, which is intoxicating and stupefying in its effects. Of course, the use of tobacco is prevalent; the Tashkendi smokes from a small gourd, brass-mounted, the tobacco being "a fine, dark-green powder." Opium is not much used, but a narcotic called *bang*, made of Indian hemp, is smoked.

The Central Asians appear to have but few of those recreations with which most nations beguile their leisure. Their favorite pastimes are those in which their horses perform a part, for everywhere fondness for the horse is a conspicuous trait. Yet they adopt many methods of passing away the time with which the rest of mankind is familiar, and some of which, no doubt, they have derived from their Russian conquerors. The children are seen playing with knuckle-bones, and the little girls nurse rather uncomely specimens of dolls. The elders play chess, cards, and dice; and they have a way of gambling, by sitting in a circle, putting down copper coins, and betting as to which coin will be the first upon which a fly will alight.

Dancing, too, is in vogue among the Central Asians, though it is supposed to be forbidden by the sacred laws of the Koran. Of music of a certain tedious, monotonous sort, they appear to be very fond, the principal instruments being two, three, or four stringed guitars, and tambourines made of goat-skins. They have also rude clarinets, trumpets, and drums. The dances are for the most part performed in private, and by *batchas*, or dancing-boys. These boys are held in high esteem in Khokand and Bokhara, where they seem, indeed, to be almost worshipped. They are addressed in terms as high-flown as "your majesty," and as they pass through the bazaars are humbly saluted by the stall-keepers. An aristocrat in Turkistan does not regard his household as complete without a *batcha*, and always has a *bazem*, or dance, performed when he gives a party or feast.

The customs of Turkistan as to courtship and marriage have many features of interest. The marriage tie is, of course, loose and unequal among a semicivilized, rather gross Mohammedan people. A man of Tashkend or Samarkand is permitted by sacred and by civil law to wed four wives. More he cannot have, unless, indeed, he choose to divorce one of those he has already; and the law of divorce there is conveniently liberal. A man may divorce himself from any of his wives by merely declaring his wish to do so, and by returning the lady her dowry and the money which he himself settled upon her at marriage. On the other hand a man must consent to a divorce if either of his wives simply requests it. All she has to do is to tell him she wishes to marry a man who is better than he.

There are certain epithets, which, if a man use them to his wife, entitles her to a divorce. The wives of the Turkistanee are regarded as his inferiors and servitors, and the instruments of his pleasures, and not as his equals; but it is sometimes found that, as in Hindostan, the wife acquires, by superior intelligence, control over her husband. It is creditable to this people that they give some education, at least, to their girls, though it is far inferior to that received by the boys. The women of warm climes like Turkistan mature at a much earlier age than those of northern and colder countries. A Turkistanee woman of thirty is old and homely. Girls are therefore regarded as quite marriageable when they are eleven or twelve, and are turning the corner of old-maidhood at twenty.

Pride of race and rank and a prudent eye for worldly goods operate in much the same manner in regard to marriages in Tashkend and Khokand as in France. Matches are made by the female relatives of the would-be bridegroom, in negotiation with those of the destined bride. Perhaps the existence of mutual love, or the probabilities of marital happiness, are less often discussed at these conferences in the women's court than matters of social standing and pecuniary resource. If these are satisfactorily arranged the marriage goes forward.

The results of the Russian occupation of the Hordes and Khanates of Turkistan cannot be regarded as wholly beneficial to the native population. The government which has been substituted for that of the Khans is military in character and operation. The governors are military officers; the laws are executed by troops. It is true that in certain respects the Russians have been wise enough to imitate the sagacious policy pursued by the English in India. Here and there material improvements have been made, such as the building of roads and bridges, and attempts to stimulate the productiveness and commercial spirit of the Khanates. Order, too, of a certain sort, has been substituted on the upper banks of the Oxus and the Jaxartes for the almost perpetual wars, civil and foreign, which have for centuries disturbed the peace of Khokand, Bokhara, and East Turkistan.

But this order is enforced by a capricious and oppressive military authority, over which the home government has practically no control whatever, and which has in return burdened the people with very heavy taxes. The native religion is protected, as are the Hindoo and Mussulman sects in India, and the Russians have gone so far in this direction as to prohibit the efforts of Christian missionaries. The Russians have here and there improved the sanitary condition of the towns, have established systems of cleaning the streets, and hospitals for the sick. But they have done very little in the way of introducing general education, though some slight effort has been made to set up schools in Samarkand and Tashkend.

The Russians seem to have been led into the mistake of trying to impose European institutions upon the Asiatics for which their past, and it may be said their genius, seem quite unfitted. They have introduced a system of passports which is very obnoxious to a population which is in large part roving and nomadic, and has been left free for centuries to wander over the deserts, steppes and oases. They have even made a trial of elective institutions. In Tashkend they have caused the city council and even the judges to be chosen by the settled and nomad population. The judges are in general appointed by the military executive; and one of the evils of the Russian rule is, that the laws which they are called upon to administer are being constantly changed, added to, and complicated by the whim of the Russian governors.

In spite of all these evils, however, the influence of the Russian conquests and settlements in Turkistan upon the people has doubtless been on the whole civilizing. This civilizing influence is exercised outside of the formalities and oppressions of law and government, by the contact of the natives with a body of men who, in comparison with them, are enlightened. The manners, modes of thoughts, and ideas of improvement of the Russians are imitated; and the natives receive new light in the ways of doing things, and in the pursuit alike of the business and of the pleasures of life.

VI.

MILITARY RESOURCES OF RUSSIA.

THE enormous extent of the military and naval armaments of the Czar's empire is not, perhaps, generally appreciated. Whatever may be the weakness of Russia's financial condition, it is certain that her war services are gigantic and formidable. It is a surprising but well authenticated fact that the possible strength of the Russian forces on a war footing reaches the prodigious total of 3,200,000 men; that is, more than one twenty-fourth of the entire population of European and Asiatic Russia. The Czar has besides, as will presently be shown, one of the finest naval armaments in the world, which is rapidly being increased by the addition of new and powerful war-ships.

The present system of army organization in Russia was put in operation in 1874. Briefly described, it ordains a yearly conscription, to which all able-bodied subjects of the Czar who have reached the age of twenty-one are liable. The period of service is fixed at fifteen years, of which the first six years are spent in the active army, and the remaining nine in the reserve. The reserve are only required to serve in time of war; in which event the younger men are sent to the field, while the elder are assigned to garrison duty. Aside from this provision for the regular forces, a militia, which may be called out in time of war, is constituted by all the able-bodied subjects of the Czar not already included in the army and naval forces.

There is yet another and altogether unique source from which Russia derives a considerable part of her warlike resources. This is the organization of Cossack troops. The Cossacks occupy a singular position in Russia. They are "a free race of men." They have never been subject to serfdom. They occupy certain territories by themselves, which they hold and use in common, the system being one of the true communist type. They are essentially a military race. They pay no taxes to the empire whatever, but are one and all bound to military service. The period of Cossack service in the active army is twenty-five years, and in the reserve five years longer. The Cossacks are, moreover, required to provide their equipments, arms, clothing, horses at their own expense. The Cossacks of the Don — the most redoubtable of all — not only pay no imposts to the Imperial collectors, but receive annual tributes, and their widows and orphans are provided with grants of land.

The Russian army report for 1884 reveals the following figures: The active army, comprising infantry, riflemen, cavalry, artillery, horse batteries and engineers, is put down at 532,000 (in round numbers) on a peace footing, and 986,000 on a war footing. The reserve is stated to contain 69,000 on a peace footing, and 563,000 on a war footing. The subsidiary services, of Cossacks, depot, local and instruction troops, and irregulars, being added to the active army and the reserve, bring the grand total of the forces to 730,000 men on a peace footing, and 1,875,000 on a war footing.

To this grand total must still be added certain special corps, and the great body of the militia, which completes the already stated number of 3,200,000 men which it is possible for the Czar to summon to his aid in case of war. The little army of Finland, about 5,000 men, is also available to the Czar in case of need. It may be worth while to add that the Cossack troops supply in all 50,000 on a peace footing and 140,000 on a war footing, the valiant Cossacks of the Don contributing the larger number and the better quality.

The Russian navy has made within the past few years, and is still making, rapid strides. Russia has, indeed, two powerful navies. One is stationed in the Baltic, and the other in the Black Sea. The Baltic fleet consisted, in 1884, of 33 armor-clad war-ships, 95 torpedo craft, 49 unarmored frigates, corvettes and clippers, 15 gunboats and 10 transports, in all 209 vessels. The Black Sea fleet comprised 7 armor-clads and 91 unarmored vessels, in all 98 vessels. There are, besides, flotillas on the Caspian, the

Sea of Aral, the Oxus and the Jaxartes, and on the Siberian coast.

The most famous of Russian war-ships — indeed, one of the most famous war-ships in the world — is the "Peter the Great." It is a monster of naval prowess. Its armor is 14 inches thick at the water-line. It has over 8,000 horse-power. Its tonnage is nearly 1,000. Its length is 330 feet, extreme breadth 69 feet, and mean draught 26 feet. But Russia is now (1885) building five new turret ships, three of which will be yet more formidable than the "Peter the Great." These are the "Tchesma," "Sinope," and "Catherine II." The other two, the "Admiral Nakhimoff" and "Alexander II.," will be only a little inferior in size and capacity.

The naval force of Russia comprises about 25,000 sailors, with 29 admirals, vice-admirals and rear-admirals, 404 captains, and 934 lieutenants and midshipmen. The sailors are obtained, like the troops, by conscription and recruitment. They serve nine years, seven in the active service, and two in the reserve.

VII.

AFGHANISTAN.

BETWEEN the territories dominated by Russia in Turkistan and the limits of the Anglo-Indian empire, lies as the sole remaining barrier separating the two great rival powers — the kingdom of Afghanistan. A brief account of Afghanistan, therefore, upon whose soil the final collision between Russia and England is altogether likely to take place, is essential to a clear idea of their mutual attitude. Afghanistan is a wild, mountainous country, though a considerable portion of its western territory comprises desert wastes. On the north the giant snow-crowned range of the Hindoo Koosh, the continuation of the Himalayas, interposes an impenetrable screen between the Khanates and Cabool, which is the chief division of Afghanistan. Cabool, with the capital of the same name, is situated on lofty table-lands, which slope gradually southward.

On the east the range of the Soliman mountains rises as a barrier on the side of India, and overlooks the broad plains of the Punjab and the almost level valley of the Indus. In the south-west a vast sand desert stretches away towards the Persian frontier, dotted here and there by inhabited oases. The north-west, — the region where the Russian and Afghan outposts confront each other — reveals successions of mountain ranges of a less height than the Hindoo Koosh, varied by arid plains, and pierced by the two valleys of the Heri and the Murghab. It is important to note that, from the table-lands and mountain barriers of Eastern Afghanistan, only two passes lead to the Punjab and the Indus valley. These are the Khyber pass, formed by the Cabool river, and farther to the south, the Bolàn pass, by which access is had to the Indian principality of Scinde.

This wild, broken, difficult and often dreary

domain of Afghanistan is inhabited by a race possessing strongly marked traits. The Afghans, who are perhaps of mixed Persian and Turcoman blood, are fierce, restless, and warlike. Powerful and rugged in frame, with rude, stern features, they are for the most part nomadic in habit, and brigands and outlaws by nature. Afghanistan, like Turkistan, has been for centuries the scene of furious feuds and bloody wars, the theatre of the intrigues and rivalries of ambitious chiefs and princes, and of frequent desolation by civil strife. Yet the country teems with the possibilities of a high material prosperity. Some of the Afghan valleys are richly fertile, and readily yield abundant harvests of useful products. Cotton and sugar can be grown in the valleys of the Cabool and its tributaries. The oases of the deserts are sometimes dense with the date-palm. Grapes, apricots, apples, pears, plums, cherries, corn, aromatic herbs, rhubarb, tobacco, pomegranates and oranges abound in the sunny lowlands. Iron and copper, too, are plentiful in certain Afghan districts.

Afghanistan was formerly subject to Persian

rule. It was not until within a century and a half that it became an independent nation. The first native dynasty was founded as recently as about 1750, by Ahmed Khan. In 1823 Dost Mohammed, a prince of remarkable energy and warlike prowess, seized the Afghan throne. By this time the English had begun to see the importance of securing their Indian dominions on its western side. Dost Mohammed fought the Persians, whom he compelled to relinquish Herat. Soon after, his aggressions towards India compelled the governor-general to invade Cabool. A small English army penetrated the country by the Bolan pass, took Candahar, and advanced and seized the city of Cabool itself. Akbar, the son of Dost Mohammed, by an act of treachery caused the entire British force, including the women and children, to be massacred as they defiled through the Khyber pass on their way back to India. Only one man of the 26,000 who had entered Afghanistan escaped this wholesale slaughter.

The English hastened to avenge the savage butchery. Again Afghanistan was invaded by

Anglo-Indian troops by both passes, Candahar and Cabool were once more taken, and Akbar's force was routed and dispersed. The army then returned to India. But the troubles with the fierce Afghans were not yet ended. They allied themselves with the rebellious Sikhs of the Punjab in 1846; but after a long desultory warfare, Dost Mohammed, who had gone to the aid of the Sikhs, was defeated in the battle of Gujerat, and driven beyond the Indus. Dost died in 1863, and his son, Shere Ali, succeeded to the throne. There now arose a fierce contention between Shere Ali and his brothers, who disputed his right to the sceptre. The British in India resolved to acquire as much influence as possible in Afghanistan as a policy of protection to India itself, recognized, supported and even helped Shere Ali in his struggle to maintain his rule.

The result was that he at last reduced the rival claimants to submission, and that the English secured a sort of alliance with the Ameer. This was sealed by the meeting of Shere Ali with the Earl of Mayo, the Viceroy, in great show and ceremony, at Umballa in 1869. Shere Ali proved to be an able and vigorous sovereign. He seems to have at first accepted in good faith the assurances and friendly offices of the Viceroy, and even proposed to send an Afghan army to check the Russian advance in Bokhara. But, later, he yielded to the seductions of Russian intrigue. The Viceroy took prompt measures to recover his influence in Afghanistan. An embassy, which assumed almost the character of a military expedition, proceeded, in 1879, to Cabool. Then the tragedy of 1840 was repeated. Cavagnari, the English leader, was massacred, with his followers, in the Afghan capital. An English army at once crossed the Indus, and once more Candahar and Cabool were taken. Shere Ali was deposed, and soon after died.

Ayoub, the son of Shere Ali, was an energetic and ambitious prince. He was at one time Governor of Herat, and by his military qualities had won the affections of many of his father's subjects. He had given Shere Ali much trouble throughout his reign by his rebellious disposition. Ayoub was hostile to English influence.

When, therefore, the English took Cabool, they excluded Ayoub from the throne, and placed upon it Abdurrahman Khan, a nephew of Shere Ali. Abdurrahman is the present Ameer of Afghanistan.

Ever since his accession there has been a diplomatic rivalry between Russia and England to gain Abdurrahman's alliance. The Russians have employed all the machinery of intrigue, secret agents, liberal expenditure of bribes, and alluring promises to gain this object; but English influence has remained from first to last predominant at Cabool, and has doubtless become yet stronger as a result of the meeting of Abdurrahman and Lord Dufferin, the Viceroy, at Kawalpindi in the early days of April, 1885. On the other hand, Ayoub Khan, the legitimate heir of Shere Ali, is still living in Persia, is not forgotten by the Afghans, and is believed to be an ardent adherent of Russia.

HERAT.

The military and strategic importance of Herat, the " Gate of India," has always been recognized both by the semi-barbaric Turcoman, Persian and Afghan, and by England and Russia. Situated at an altitude of 2,500 feet above the sea on the river Heri; standing at the junction of the great valleys which lead from Persia on the west and north-west, of the Merv oasis and Turkistan on the north, and of the valleys which approach the Afghan fortresses on the east, its value in military operations cannot easily be overestimated. It is Herat upon which the covetous eyes both of the Russian and the Englishman have long been fixed. Its possession by one or by the other would be the first checkmate in the mighty game of war in which they should engage.

Herat is about 400 miles from Askabad on the Caspian, 350 from Cabool, 300 from Candahar, and rather over 400 from Quettah, which is the nearest point actually garrisoned by Anglo-Indian troops, and which commands the Bolan pass. Herat was long the seat of the descendants of Timour Tamerlane. It has always been bitterly fought for by the neighboring races. It has been the object of many desperate sieges.

In 1857 an English force of 35,000, with fifty pieces of artillery, was kept at bay before its ramparts for ten months by its Afghan defenders. The English have long looked upon Herat as the outpost of their Oriental empire against Russian aggression; and this fact has given rise to the wars between England and Persia, the latter State having been for years completely subject to Russian influence.

The military importance of Herat may be somewhat judged when it is known that not only do all the roads into the Indian peninsula lead to and from this famous stronghold, but that its defences are of a most elaborate kind. It is a fortified city of quadrangular shape, surrounded by ditch and wall, and commanded by a strong citadel on its northern side. Its ramparts consist of a series of artificial hills of an average height of ninety feet, supported by counter-forts of masonry with round towers, and crested with a wall thirty-two feet high. The deep ditch below, supplied by never-failing water, girds this enormous rampart, which dominates all the surrounding district.

The neighborhood of Herat can supply everything needful for a great army, even to lead and saltpetre ; and the population, which, it is conjectured, could without much difficulty be drawn away from Afghan affiliations, is numerous, warlike, and readily bought. " From Herat," says an English authority, " the Cossack can practically command Khorassan, Balkh, and Maimena. At Herat he sits at the natural gate-house of India ; for though the passes lie farther east and south, here is the outwork of the peninsula which looks into them all. Russia at Herat means Russia the master of Afghanistan ; and the master of the upper plateau of Afghanistan, commanding access to the passes from the north, is in fact the master of India."

The testimony of Sir Henry Rawlinson, a profound student of the region, as to the importance of Herat, is well worth being heard. More than fifteen years ago this eminent geographer declared : " Russia will assuredly some day draw that final parallel from Askabad on the south-east corner of the Caspian, along the Persian frontier to Herat. Established on such a line, her position would indeed be formidable. Troops, stores and material might be concentrated to any extent at Askabad. The country between that port and Herat is open and admirably supplied. A line of military posts would connect the two positions, and effectually control the Turcomans, thereby conferring an essential benefit on Persia, and securing her good-will and coöperation. Herat has been often called ' the Key of India,' and fully deserves its reputation as the most important military position in Central Asia. The earthworks which surround the town are of the most colossal character, and might be strengthened indefinitely. Water and supplies abound, and routes from all the great cities to the north, which would furnish the Russian supports, meet in this favored spot.

"In fact, it is no exaggeration to say that if Russia were once established in full strength at Herat, and her communications were secured in one direction with Askabad through Meshed, in another with Khiva through Merv, and in a third with Tashkend and Bokhara through Mymeneh and the passage of the Oxus, all the forces of Asia would be inadequate to expel her from the position. Supposing, too, that she were bent on mischief— and it is only hostility to England that would be likely to lead her into so advanced and menacing a position — she would have the means of seriously injuring us; since, in addition to her own forces, the unchallenged occupation of Herat would place the whole military resources of Persia and Afghanistan at her disposal."

VIII.

ENGLAND VERSUS RUSSIA.

MANY conjectures have been expressed by eminent writers on Eastern questions as to the real purpose of Russia in extending her dominions southward in Central Asia. Some of these are bold in their belief that Russia meditates the conquest, sooner or later, of India itself. Some are of opinion that Russia is simply seeking an outlet for her commerce in the southern Asiatic seas. Some are confident that her chief object is to control the vast commerce of China, and indeed of all Asia. Some think that territorial greed and the ambition to found a great Asiatic empire lie at the bottom of her proceeding. Some suspect that the ancient Russian aspiration to possess Constantinople impels the aggression; that she either intends to approach the capital of the Caliph from the Asiatic side, or to be in a position to overawe India, and so at an opportune moment to compel the assent of England to her occupation of the long-coveted city.

Another suggestion has recently been made why Russia may be willing, in spite of her desperate financial condition and her shattered credit, to enter upon a great war. It is hinted that the wide discontent which prevails throughout European Russia at the rule of the Czar, revealed by the hidden conspiracy and fitfully daring deeds of the Nihilists, influences the Czar and his advisers to think that perhaps a war would distract the minds of his subjects from their oppressions, and unite the people in an absorption in a great thrilling event. Such a policy on the part of tyrants who have been beset with similar dangers in their internal government has again and again been repeated in history. Both the Napoleons resorted to foreign war as a safety-valve for the growing disaffection of their subjects.

It is a very wide-spread if not the prevailing opinion in England, that the presence of Russia in Central Asia means at least three of the purposes above indicated. Many Englishmen fully believe that Russia proposes to approach near enough to India to impose a check upon England in the East, and thus, by tying the hands of her traditional rival, be enabled to undertake that conquest of Constantinople which was the dream of Peter the Great, and the failure to accomplish which broke the heart of the austere and haughty Nicholas; that she also hopes, at some time or other, to avail herself of a revolt among the Hindoo provinces from English rule, to enter her wedge of intrigue, bribery, and promises, following this up by the actual invasion of India; and thirdly, in the meanwhile, to obtain for herself the monopoly of Oriental trade.

It is true that Mr. Schuyler, probably the best informed of American writers on the subject, declares, in his "Turkistan," that these English theories of the Russian advance in Central Asia are fallacious. He says that "Russia has no plot to dominate the whole of Asia, nor has she any settled intention of making an attack on India, nor even any desire for the possession of India." He attributes the Russian encroachments to "yearly and almost daily changing circumstances;" yet he thinks that, in the case of war between Russia and England, and if Russia found it practicable to make a diversion on India, she would not probably hesitate to do so. Indeed, Mr. Schuyler himself points out that the Czar Paul proposed a joint invasion of India to the first Napoleon, and that such a design was also seriously entertained, early in his reign, by the Czar Nicholas.

Nine years have elapsed, however, since Mr. Schuyler's very able work was written; and during these nine years many things have happened. The events which have since taken place serve to provide some further material for surmising what Russia's purposes really are. The acquisition of the Merv oasis certainly was not needed to preserve the Russian outposts on the Oxus from attack, nor did the excuse that the frontier must be protected exist to justify that proceeding. The evident desire of Russia to possess Herat can only be explained on the supposition that she has other objects than merely to secure the dominion of Turkistan which she has acquired. It is a desire prompted by a policy of aggression, not by one of protection and defence. And the fact that in Herat Russia seeks to hold "the Gate of India" has a significance which did not necessarily apply to the conquest of the Khanates, the domination of the Oxus valley, or the occupation of Merv and Sarakhs.

From all the circumstances revealed in the course of Russia's movements, and from her present attitude, it is surely not an unfair assumption that the three objects with which she is credited by enlightened Englishmen are really those which she at least has in contemplation, if they are not those which she has definitely decided to pursue. It is not too much to believe of an ambitious, covetous and still semi-barbaric régime, like that of the Czars, that it is aiming at a threefold purpose; that it seeks a military, a political and a commercial advantage in its Oriental advance. It is highly probable that Russia aims to found her Oriental empire on a broader base; to gain access for her fleets and merchant marine in the south Asiatic seas; to secure such a footing as to checkmate the ancient opposition of England to her designs on Turkey; and to command the old highways and establish new ones, by which she can acquire exclusive control of Oriental trade.

That her policy bears a commercial as well as a military aspect is apparent from her activity in restoring and regulating the great emporiums of Turkistan, and the steps she has taken, as fast as her conquests were made, to establish commercial depots and afford protection for caravans. Her commercial policy, too, is evidently twofold. She wishes to monopolize the market of such thriving cities as Bokhara, Kashgar, Yarkand and Samarkand for Russian manufactures, thus replacing the trade in English manufactures *via* India; and she wishes to possess and guard a direct highway of communication between her European dominions and China. She has gone far on her way to accomplish both these objects; but her task is not yet completed, and, as its area narrows, the struggle to complete it must become more and more bitter. England is waking up to the very serious danger of losing, at the very least, the monopoly of that Oriental commerce which is one of the main advantages of holding India, and for which the possession of India has given her large facilities.

But, whether it is Russia's purpose to pursue all or only one of the objects suggested, in any case she distinctly threatens the interests, the prestige and the power of England in the East. Her presence on the frontier, and, much more, within the territory of Afghanistan, must be a perpetual menace to the British empire. No trust can be reposed by English statesmen in Russian assurances, promises, or even treaties. Again and again have Russian duplicity and bad faith been rudely demonstrated to confiding premiers and secretaries of state. More than ever is it clear that the only reliance England has for the defence of her position in the East, and the success of her policy of safe-guarding India as well in Europe and Africa as in India itself, is upon that disciplined valor of the British soldiery which has never yet faltered, and upon the prodigious wealth which British thrift and energy have accumulated in generations of enterprise, colonization and sturdy toil.

This even the most peacefully inclined of English statesmen are beginning to perceive. It is recognized that in order to hold the magnificent dependency of India, and to preserve the proud city of the Bosphorus, England and Russia must sooner or later clinch in what will probably be a colossal conflict; and those who would see the semi-barbaric races of the most ancient continent receive an Anglo-Saxon rather than a semi-Tartaric civilization will, in that event, bid God-speed to the arms of our mother isle.

THE END.

www.ingramcontent.com/pod-product-compliance
Lightning Source LLC
Chambersburg PA
CBHW020108170426
43199CB00009B/442